C000120952

Becoming a Servant Leader

Becoming a Servant Leader

*The Art of Unlocking the Abilities of
Others to Get Things Done*

John Rodgers

Copyright © 2017 – John Rodgers

All rights reserved. No part of this book may be used or reproduced in any manner, stored in a retrieval system, or transmitted in any form or by any means—electronic, mechanical, photocopy, recording, scanning or any other—except in the case of brief quotations in printed reviews, without the prior written permission from the author.

Dale Carnegie® is a registered trademark of the Dale Carnegie Training organization founded in 1912 and focused on self-improvement with offices worldwide.

Scotland Media Group
3583 Scotland Road
Building 70
Scotland PA 17254

Book ISBN: 978-1-941746-38-7
eBook ISBN: 978-1-941746-39-4

For Worldwide Distribution, Printed in the United States

1 2 3 4 5 6 7 / 21 20 19 18 17

Dedication

To my wife, Colleen, who suspended a career in her chosen field to serve our five children, which was helpful to me, us, and our five children: Alexandra, Jackie, Sam, Jillian, and Kaitrin. A true example of a servant heart for which I will always be forever grateful.

Contents

Contents

Introduction

There is a choice you have to make, in everything you do.
So keep in mind that in the end, the choice you make,
makes you. –Anonymous

Where did it all start—this passion that I have developed for Servant Leadership? Well, like most things in life that are lasting, it's a process not an event. However, events can be turning points that get our attention and start us down the right path. The following are two significant events that stand out in my life.

In the middle of my personal leadership crisis, Bob Allen, my sales manager, called me while I was driving into Pittsburgh; I was on the parkway, late on a Tuesday afternoon. He said, "John, I just got a call from one of our top customers saying they are looking for a senior executive to coach an international senior executive who is part of a team that has just taken over an organization…and English is not the executive's primary language." The challenge: he is giving a major talk in Phoenix to customers and vendors, laying out the vision for the new company and why their parent company decided to purchase our client. He has thirty minutes to present the case. He also has nearly 200 slides—and his last presentation did not go so well.

As a Dale Carnegie® franchisee, I, of course, replied, "Tell him to enroll in the Dale Carnegie Course," and hung up. This was not a response from a Servant Leader. At the time, I thought I was a Servant Leader, but I really had no clue. In fact, I actually thought I was being helpful to everyone involved. Little did I know that within four months I would be in a leadership think tank that would launch me into a personal journey of self-discovery, in parallel with a new professional passion for executive coaching.

Event 1

Fortunately Bob called back, and I took on the assignment of being this international leader's presentation coach. Before I met the executive, I sat through two hours of pre-training on executive protocol with international executives. How to bow, hold a business card, and if he dismissed me, to bow, thank, and leave immediately. Finally the training was over and I was ushered into a large conference room. There I noticed a PowerPoint presentation preloaded with what I assumed was my task for the evening. Then I waited and waited…finally a door opened and in walked a much younger executive than I imagined; with a sleepy grin he said, "Good evening, you must be John?"

Then life took over, just two guys establishing trust, respect, and credibility. I remember asking, "So how did you get selected to come to Pittsburgh?" The young executive responded, "I think because I speak the best English." We both laughed, and got started. We spent two evenings together. I reduced his slide show to 50, with one 20-second video. I never saw him again, but I did hear that his presentation was tremendous with great customer feedback. Today, almost ten years later, he is Chief Operating Officer (COO) of the parent company.

Because of this small success, a week later I received a call from the same Human Resources (HR) professional who had called me previously. This time the request was for me to coach a senior executive who was recently promoted into a global role. I accepted, and this assignment launched me into a journey of executive coaching that would change my life. More about this assignment later in the book.

Event 2

The second significant event took place in my business. Right before my eyes I watched a business shift happen that would force me to make some tremendous mental changes if I was going to survive and thrive as a business person. As a result, I allowed myself to have an encounter with Kevin Crone who was the Dale Carnegie franchisee in Toronto, Canada. Kevin was a generation older, very successful, but was always trying new things to meet the market's demands. To me, his ventures were just as flat-out confusing and threatening. However, with a business downturn, I was ready to listen. The old Chinese proverb rang true: "When the student is ready, the teacher will come."

During this period, I was elected to the International Dale Carnegie Franchise Association (IDCFA) Board of Directors. The Board was meeting in Chicago for three days to find answers regarding the economic downturn of 2009. Kevin Crone was asked to facilitate the meetings. For the first time, I actually sat, really listened, and began to understand that perhaps I needed a paradigm (pattern or standard) shift to lead, think, and work differently.

This guy who I thought was crazy was maybe actually wise. He asked me what I thought my customers were motivated to buy and then had the gall to ask if my current offerings were what the customers wanted. In a dramatic way, he was suggesting it wasn't about my likes and desires, but the people who actually paid my bills. All these years I was just saying and believing I was a Servant Leader, but with no real understanding of how to be a Servant Leader. Furthermore, if I was just about building an enduring business to win awards, my current reality was off course.

My first task after the Chicago meeting was to send Kevin my company vision statement. I was so proud of my vision; it spoke of all my aspirations of being the number one Dale Carnegie franchise on planet Earth. Kevin read it and called me almost immediately. I remember taking the call in my office. My first thought was that he must really be blown way because he is calling me back so quickly.

Kevin said, "John, is this it?" in a rather flat, nonexcited tone.

"Well, yea," I replied. Then the next words out of his mouth rocked my world.

"What! Are you in kindergarten?"

After I picked myself up off the floor, he challenged me: If I thought my vision was so great, I was to set up an appointment with my top customers and see how inspired they were to make me the top Dale Carnegie franchise in the world.

Then it hit me—hard. It's not about me and my business; in fact, it can't be about me at all. Instead, it must be about others. My first intellectual experience in understanding why shifting from "me" to "we" was so vitally important.

However, converting it from a thought into action was a process. I had no idea how long it would take, and I'm still working at making it a reality every day. The concept is simple— focus on others, not myself. The challenge: that concept goes against almost every survival thought process I've learned since birth. Furthermore, I must survive to be of any value to others. I wondered, *I want to create a relentless pursuit of personal growth on behalf of servicing others, while becoming the biggest fan of their success.*

Sounds wonderful, but let's be real, that is not the world we live in. Most of us live in a world of individual competition and the only score card is how we feel and our net worth. Teamwork, collaboration, shared revenue, having each other's back sounds like baseball, hot dogs, apple pie, and Chevrolet. Throw in a cold Coke—who can be against that on a hot, summer day?

But what if we turn the leadership paradigm upside down? Instead of others existing for our success, we exist to help others succeed. This book is a guide to becoming a Servant Leader.

The coaching stories I share throughout the book are true to the point I am making; but to be fair to past and future coaching clients, the names of individuals and companies have been changed unless I have received specific written permission.

This book walks you through the process of shifting your leadership mindset from a "control mindset" to a "helpful mindset." Some philosophical thinking is necessary, but I trust you will find the real value in this book is in the "how" and the actions and steps to take to become a Servant Leader.

This book is my journey to becoming a Servant Leader as a business owner and an executive coach. My life, business, coaches, personal discoveries, and the men and women I coached from 2008 through to the present have helped mold me, my thinking, and my progress in becoming a Servant Leader. The journey continues every day from the time I wake up—it's an exciting trip. Enjoy the read.

Onward!

Note: The content in the book is designed for easy reading and comprehension, complete with important bullet points, relevant graphs, and poignant quotes as memory glue. Each chapter concludes with Key Questions that will stir your thoughts toward introspection as well as spark a larger perspective of your leadership capabilities.

It is suggested to keep a notepad and pen (or laptop) nearby when reading so you can jot down ideas, tactics, and information that you can either put into practice immediately, or develop into a long-term strategy for becoming the leader you envision. Writing your answers to the Key Questions will give you a record that you can refer to after reading the book. You can also keep track of your progress by recording milestones and accomplishments along your journey to *Becoming a Servant Leader.*

CHAPTER 1

Why Become a Servant Leader?

Do things for others and you will find your
self-consciousness evaporating like morning dew
on a Missouri cornfield in July. –Dale Carnegie

I'm frequently asked, "Why should I embrace the role of Servant Leader? It's 180-degrees opposite of what I've been taught about management." My long answer, "Being a Servant Leader brings all aspects (roles) of your life into sublime alignment and balance! Imagine:

- At Home – Your family loves you. You are a great provider. Your family has fun together and solve problems together. Your children earn good grades and have lots of good friends. All is well at home.
- At Work – You are a rising star in the company. Everyone wants to be on your team. Your employees would run through a blazing fire if you asked them to. Together your team is one of the tops in the company and getting better every day. All is well at work.
- At Leisure – You have many good friends. Your social calendar is full, everyone wants you at their event because you are always positive and upbeat. You have the energy to enjoy life and feel great. All is well in leisure.
- At Peace – You are comfortable with who you are and what you are doing. Your stress level is low because everything is under control. You are at peace.

This sounds like an incredible life, doesn't it? It's more like a dream in a movie sequence than anything that could happen in reality. Right? There was a time I thought so as well. Let me share how Servant Leadership has transformed and is transforming my life.

My Story

In the fall of 2008, my business was in trouble. My credit was overextended, traditional revenues that in the past were predictable were now questionable at best, and I was going to have to put more dollars from personal savings into the business checking account to meet payroll. I had been an award-winning Dale Carnegie franchise owner since 2001. You would think that after seven years, I would have had enough experience to successfully navigate through the storms of daily business challenges—but instead I hit a wall. I was so frustrated, so disappointed, so embarrassed, and frankly, scared. What I used to do for fun and enjoyment was no longer fun due to the stress of the circumstances. In fact, my career was a drudgery. It was so easy to play the blame game, to build myself up by pointing to others' failings as the reason for my pending doom.

To make matters worse, I was elected to the International Dale Carnegie Franchise Association (IDCFA) board of directors and was expected to provide leadership to the global franchisees in our network of about 180 members. This was also the time when our five teenagers were beginning to go off to college. I needed a turnaround, and I needed to find some answers in a hurry. Sound familiar?

Thanks to great coaching, I discovered the problem was *me*. I had built a business on my pending success and happiness, and then discovered in the fall of 2008 it was not about me. I needed to make a paradigm shift and focus on others in every area of my life. At best I was a Level II (top-down) leader. As you will soon discover, I thought that operating at Level III (buddy/boss) was actually being a servant, when I actually had no idea what a

Servant Leader (Level V) was. Imagine my shock to discover I was causing distrust and confusion in my own organization. (The Five Levels of Leadership is explained in a chart later in this chapter.)

I remember the day when I stood in my office in downtown Pittsburgh looking out at the city with tears in my eyes, knowing what I wanted to create, a Dale Carnegie franchise that was truly about helping our customers and associates win, while coming to grips with my current reality—that we were functioning almost at the opposite of what I wanted to create. Back then, looking at those first action steps on the flip chart to get us from where we were to where we wanted to be seemed impossible. The pain came when I realized the truth that to create a company that was going to be about others, I needed to fix *me* first.

Action one: my mindset needed to change from "me" to "we." So, I started a journey one step at a time and rediscovered Dale Carnegie teaching through the eyes of a Servant Leader who genuinely desires to be helpful rather than controlling. I assure you it's a process not an event, and it has been the hardest shift I have ever had to make as a leader. That is why I can truly say today that I am still learning how to become a Servant Leader.

The results of my shift in thinking and leading have been nothing short of miraculous. My team and I made a fundamental shift in meeting our customers' wants and needs, which turned around our current and future financial status. We could pay off debt, restructure our leadership team, sell two franchises and then buy an additional franchise territory and plan for sustainable growth. Yes, we are still investing, but what a difference when "we" invest with a roadmap and a plan rather than just "me" trying to avoid disaster or thinking that others might be impressed with my success. Remember, it's not the awards on your shelf that build a legacy, it's the people you helped build who will perpetuate your legacy long after you pass from this planet.

One business surprise in making this shift was a new offering of executive coaching. Because of my successes *and* failings as a

Servant Leader, I am a better executive coach. My focus is helping leaders at all levels of an organization by encouraging them to genuinely see the world from others' points of view, which is helpful in accomplishing and achieving their goals through the good times and the challenging times.

Servant leadership is a process, not an event. It is the process of becoming helpful to others. As a leader, the process is to be useful in helping others achieve personal and professional outcomes that they would not have accomplished on their own. A Servant Leader sees the world through a paradigm of being helpful rather than being controlling. This is accomplished daily or hourly by choosing to wear servant lenses. Once you intentionally start wearing those lenses, you will never again think, work, or play the same.

> *The simple outcome of Servant Leadership is to unlock the abilities of others to get things done.*

As a business leader, in my experience it's almost impossible to be a perfect Servant Leader 100 percent of the time. So to help you on your journey, look for moments or seasons of times when you exercise Servant Leadership tendencies. Perhaps an analogy will help. Suppose I created an app that you could wear around your wrist like an iWatch and it documented which level of leadership you were talking, planning, or thinking from; in fact, it converted a time log in percentages. Your goal would be to improve the amount of time you chose to function as a Servant Leader. For example, when my granddaughter, Reagan, was running toward the street pushing mini-mouse in her little stroller, I turned into a complete Level I Controlling Dictator.

Let's dig in. The following is a simple chart that we will refer to as we walk through the book. These levels were first introduced to me by one of my coaches, Rod Bartell and his organization. It clearly depicts the levels of leadership and the relationships between leaders and those they lead.

5 Levels of Leadership

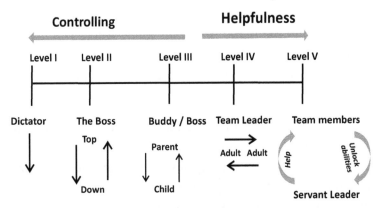

Overview of Servant Leadership

I came across the following story by an unknown author while preparing for a Chamber of Commerce presentation in Chambersburg, Pennsylvania. It humorously reveals how truly transparent some leaders can be. Notice the "self-focus" versus the "other-focus" in what is inferred and not even spoken.

Perspective: Different Leadership Positions

A man is flying in a hot air balloon and realizes he is lost. He descends a bit and spots a man down below. He lowers the balloon farther and shouts, "Excuse me, can you tell me where I am?"

The man below says, "Yes, you're in a hot air balloon, hovering thirty feet above this field. You are between forty and forty-two degrees' North latitude and between fifty-eight and sixty degrees' West longitude."

"You must work in information technology," says the balloonist.

"I do," replies the man, "but how did you know?"

"Well," says the balloonist, "everything you have told me is technically correct, but it's of no use to me."

The man below says, "You must be a corporate senior manager."

"I am," replies the balloonist, "but how did you know?"

"Well," says the man, "You don't know where you are or where you're going, but you expect me to be able to help. You're in the same position you were before we met, but now it's my fault."

Question: Why is servant leadership the preferred style? There are four answers:

One: It's the only leadership level that has the potential of producing successful long-term, sustainable business and financial results. If you take the long view and want to build a legacy, becoming a Servant Leader gives you the competitive edge.

Two: The generational shift the world and the United States in particular are experiencing almost mandates that we work hard at changing our leadership tendencies. For example, "millennials—those born between the years of 1980 and 1996— were projected to number 75.3 million by 2015. The generation continues to grow through additions to the population through immigration. Trends that are discussed in relation to millennials include the facts that they are racially diverse, relatively unattached to organized politics and religion, linked by social media, burdened by debt—especially student loan debt— distrustful of people, and in no rush to get married, but otherwise they're optimistic about the future."[1] This group will absolutely abandon a Level I, II, and III leader. They do not want a mom or dad; they want a leader. In fact, it's no longer about what you are going to give workers—it's now more important to help them see and understand who is going to lead them. It's not *what,* but *who!*

Three: Servant leadership is now about worldwide competition and being able to compete in global markets—not just neighboring towns or states. Yes, I am still a fan of process improvement, but the next costs and revenue breakthroughs are going to be a result of how we choose to lead talent—not from incremental savings.

If you are committed to your people and believe they are your greatest resource, then you will understand that becoming more of a Servant Leader is the only proven sustainable way to truly unleash talents. You unleash talent by turning people loose, tapping into their creativity, while finding new and innovative solutions to old problems.

I had the privilege of coaching a global leader for engineering services in the energy sector. He had an operating profit and top-line revenue goals that seemed insurmountable—but he bought into becoming a servant and moving away from Level II (top-down) thinking due to his past success. One of the Servant Leader's techniques is to manage by "wandering around."[2]

One afternoon the man I was coaching conducted a roundtable discussion with employees. He listened more than talking, which was a challenge for him and the employees who were not used to talking. The meeting was quiet, with only guarded responses and seemingly little if any progress. Later he received an email from an attendee asking if he would stop by her office. The next day he dropped by and asked how he could help. The female executive looked at him and asked, "Were you serious about wanting our ideas?" After he assured he was, she told him about an idea she had for years about how to generate new revenue at a high margin. To make a long story short, her idea generated $5 million and exceeded operating profit. She was one of many who contributed to Mike's division, exceeding their goals with an enthusiastic and more engaged workforce.

Four: My final business reason to encourage all leaders to operate as Servant Leaders has to do with employee engagement. The evidence is solid that employee engagement cannot be managed it—must be led. Positive employee engagement increases because of the following three top factors:

- Relationship with immediate supervisor
- Belief in senior leadership
- Pride in working for the company[3]

Servant Leaders create the right atmosphere for all three factors to improve.

If direct improvement in the bottom-line has not convinced you, how about non-revenue reasons? Servant Leaders:

- Achieve greater work-life balance
- Reduce unsustainable stress
- Deflect business pressures
- Become better parents
- Make new and lasting friendships
- Have more enjoyable, collaborative, and passionate marriages

> *The Servant Leader's DNA is helpfulness. Their currency is trust, respect, and credibility.*

As an executive coach who has observed and talked with hundreds of executives, I can say we have a current leadership crisis—most leaders believe they are operating at a Level IV or V (like me prior to 2008). The reality is that more than 90 percent of leaders today function at a Level I & II.

For the remainder of the book we will put on our Level V Servant Leader paradigm lenses and discover how to become a Servant Leader and unleash the talents of others. Please keep reading—you will enjoy the journey.

Onward!

Summary

Why become a Servant Leader? It's the only leadership level that has the potential to produce successful long-term, sustainable business and financial results. If you take the long-term view and want to build a legacy, becoming a Servant Leader gives you the competitive edge.

Key Questions

1. *What is your story as a leader?*

2. *In what level of leadership do you think you function most time?*

3. *In what level of leadership would your subordinates and peers say you function most the time?*

4. *In what level of leadership would the people you love the most—family and close friends—say you function with them most the time?*

5. *How would everything change for you as a leader if you viewed the world through a Servant Leader lens?*

Endnotes

1. Katherine Reynolds Lewis, "Everything you need to know about your Millennial co-workers," *Fortune,* June 23, 2015; http://fortune.com/2015/06/23/know-your-millennial-co-workers/; accessed February 23, 2017.

2. Thomas J. Peters and Robert H. Waterman Jr., *In Search of Excellence* (New York: HarperCollins, 2004).

3. "What Drives Employee Engagement and Why it Matters," Dale Carnegie White Paper, (Dale Carnegie & Associates, Inc., Copyright © 2012).

CHAPTER 2

Leadership Versus Management

The goal of many leaders is to get people to think more highly of the leader. The goal of a great leader is to help people to think more highly of themselves. –J. Carla Nortcutt

To be clear, leaders lead people, and managers manage processes, systems, and activities.

Now that those words are defined, I offer this example. Colleen and I are planning a trip to Europe, and on my bucket list is to see the beaches at Normandy. D-Day was June 6, 1944, and what happened that day provides a great example of the difference between the role of a manager and a leader. When the transport boats hit the beaches and huge metal ramps dropped and the troops stormed onto the shore, I would want to run behind a leader who was sure to make progress. Then I would hope that a manager was calling in coordinates for air cover.

In business, many times we must play the dual role of manager and leader. The difference being, in my experience, individuals become much more comfortable with their role as a manager than as a leader. Successful businesses need leaders.

On the morning of one of the most famous battles fought at Gettysburg, Pickett's Charge, General Robert E. Lee rode his horse, Traveler, in front of the lines of troops and gave each group a nod and tip of his hat. Later a soldier who survived the battle commented that when General Lee rode by and tipped his hat, every man was "ready to storm the gates of hell," and they did. Leadership.

As Ford Motor Company's new CEO, it didn't take Alan Mulally long to make an obvious observation and a fundamental change. "There are too many meetings; when do you have time to think about the customer?" Mulally continued, "From now on there will only be one corporate-level meeting… Attendance is mandatory for all senior executives. Everyone is expected to personally deliver succinct status reports and updates on their progress toward the company's turnarounds goals." A Level I communication directive with a Servant Leader's heart in making changes led to one of America's greatest business turnarounds ever—without any government funding—and impacted millions of people.[1] Leadership.

John D. Rockefeller Sr. followed the numbers and accounted for every cent. He not only balanced his checkbook to the penny, but wanted a strict accounting of the cost of every employee to the penny. One story in *Titan,* his biography, states that Rockefeller did a cost analysis of food consumption by servants on his three estates that reflected a cost per servant between $6.62 and $13.35 per month. This was when Rockefeller himself had a personal income of $58 million per year, equivalent to $1 billion in today's dollars.[2] Manager.

One day I walked into a planning session of an executive I was coaching. On his whiteboard, he and a team of associates were mapping out a month-long trip to India. Meeting time schedules, flight schedules, coaching schedules, hotel accommodations, and other events. The difference in routing could alter the cost by tens of thousands of dollars. Manager.

All of these examples highlight the dual functions we have as leaders of people and as managers of processes, systems, and activities. The challenge: most executives are usually most comfortable with their management duties because either they are skilled or have had success accomplishing them in the past. Perhaps some of their management skills led to their promotions.

Management skills are more easily defined and more easily accomplished; I accomplished something tangible today. Leadership, on the other hand, takes up an extraordinary amount of time with little sense of accomplishment—plus stress.

Clint Hurdle is the manager of the Pittsburgh Pirates. Hurtle is passionate about servant leadership and actually has a plan to mentor his staff and players in servant leadership. One day we were discussing the challenges he faces in professional sports— where almost everyone is looking out only for themselves. He looked up at me and grinned and said, "John, do you know why I believe leadership is so challenging?" Obviously curious I asked, "Why?" He said, "Because people are messy." He's right.

My definition of "mentoring" is an intentional intervention into someone's life for the purpose of personal and professional development. When you begin to unpack the life piece, you better hang on and be strong enough to stand for what is right, true, and honorable. Everyone has a story. Here are just a few examples of what I have encountered while coaching executives:

- An executive lying on the hallway floor shaking due to stress
- A complete mental breakdown due to confusion on a project
- A death
- Sexual harassment that would not be dealt with by the organization
- An unjustified-perceived firing and subsequent lawsuit
- A physical illness that the employee hid due to fear of losing the job
- A president of a $70-million division broke down and sobbed for fear that the company directors would find out he was incompetent
- Having an affair with two individuals in the department
- A CEO of a global company with the emotional maturity of a teenager

- Having a racist attitude toward team members
- Broken relationships with children, spouses, and parents
- Odd beliefs

My mentor in the training business was a leader for whom I have great respect and love, Bob Spinazzola. We used to have mind-numbing conversations about a phrase he thought was a lie: "There but for the grace of God, go I." He believed and I agree to a point, we all get to make our own choices, yes. But I do believe in absolute truth, and that there is a right and wrong. I do all I can to refrain from judging others to a point. The big idea is that Servant Leaders need to be open to hear and deal with all kinds of issues—if we are truly going to be helpful to others.

The goal in servant leadership is to unleash the talents of others. Surprisingly, as we become more helpful from their point of view, the more likely we will be in achieving our goals by seeing others unleash their talents. Servant Leaders create the environment for talents to be unleashed. We want to create advancement versus isolation in achieving business and personal outcomes.

Servant Leaders influence others. We influence by impacting what others think and feel as we change beliefs and paradigms. Other leadership levels immediately focus on behavior; this can produce results, usually short-term in nature. If we are interested in *sustainable* influence, we will use evidence to influence beliefs and paradigms. Keep in mind the Servant Leader can use behavior or action to help change a belief or paradigm because we know action can change how we feel and then think. Regardless, knowing this provides many coaching opportunities.

For example, in 2012, Dale Carnegie released an on-line training course. I was greatly opposed to this idea; after all, how can someone be taught by watching a few videos what we do in the classroom with an instructor? Could the on-line course produce a life-changing experience? I sincerely doubted it. Then I had a paradigm shift.

Leadership - Influence Wheel

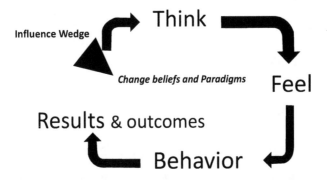

When I was delivering a leadership half-day summit, at one of the breaks a hospital executive approached me and thanked me. I was curious, and asked him to tell me why. He explained that he had recently taken a Dale Carnegie course and it changed his life. Not just with the relationships he had with his co-workers in the hospital, but what a difference it had made with him as a father at home with his eldest son.

Smiling inside I was happy to hear something we are privileged to hear a lot in our business. His next phrase floored me. He said, "It was so wonderful to have this experience and never have to leave my office." WHAT?! He had taken an on-line course and it was life-changing. Paradigm shift! Believe me, our franchises today are leading in the digital market and we hear hundreds of stories like the one I heard during the break at my leadership summit.

P.S. I asked the hospital exec who had the life-changing on-line experience, "So, how are you enjoying this morning session here at the summit?" "Oh" he said, "it's okay." Just another opportunity to remind myself it's not about me.

Onward!

Summary

You *manage* process, systems and activities—you *lead* people. The goal in servant leadership is to unleash the talents of others. Surprisingly, as we become more helpful from their point of view, the more likely we will achieve our goals by seeing others unleash their talents.

Key Questions

1. *To what degree to you confuse leadership and management?*

2. *Have you ever found yourself managing instead of leading? How was that working?*

3. *How does workplace stress affect you?*

4. *How often have you tried to influence behavior before trying to change a belief or paradigm?*

5. *How hard is it for you not to make life about your wishes desires and wants?*

Endnotes

1. Bryce Hoffman, *An American Icon* (Danvers, MA: Crown Business, 2012), 102.

2. Ron Chernow, *Titan*, (New York: Random House, 2004), 505.

CHAPTER 3

Defining Servant Leadership

Serving others breaks you free from the shackles of self and
self-absorption that choke out the joy of living.
– James C. Hunter, The Servant

Franklin Gomez was born in the Dominican Republic, raised in Puerto Rico, attended high school in Florida, and then attended Michigan State University. Franklin is a world class international Olympic wrestler. He has spent his life pursuing the dream of winning an Olympic gold medal. Although he won the college National Championship in 2009 while attending Michigan State University and then after college was a runner-up in the 2011 world competition, he competed but did not place in the London games in 2012. Finally, at age 30, he was ready to pursue his goal of winning the gold medal in Rio de Janeiro in 2016.

He won his first match then faced, in the quarterfinals, Uzbekistan's Ikhtiyor Navruzov, the 2015 world runner-up and lost a heartbreaking match 8-5. Near the end of the match, it appeared to everyone that Franklin hit a beautiful 4-point takedown to win and advance toward his goal of winning a gold medal. However, after video review, he was denied the takedown because it was ruled out of bounds, so he lost the match and his dream was shattered.

Earlier in the summer, prior to the Olympics, I met Franklin in State College, Pennsylvania, on a Sunday morning in church.

Franklin was training with the Penn State Wrestling Club. Because I am a wrestling fan, we connected right away and I learned not only of his faith walk but of his journey as a wrestler and his aspirations. He was now ready, most likely, for his final try at the Olympic Gold.

When I watched his match and saw how he lost, I was sickened that a dream could so randomly be taken away from this young man. Talk about injustice! I didn't sleep for two nights, dreading what to say when I saw him again. Little did I know how Franklin was dealing with the defeat. If I had known, I would not have lost a wink of sleep.

Two months later I saw Franklin again in church. He smiled and I asked him, "Have you recovered—how are you doing?"

He grinned and said, "John, I was over it in five minutes. I went back into the locker room and the first thing that came to mind was the Old Testament story of Joseph who was sold into slavery by his brothers and that his mistreatment, far worse than me losing a wrestling match, brought about so much goodness to others. So perhaps my mishap will bring some degree of comfort to someone else." This illustrates the mind and heart of Servant Leaders—when they are disappointed or frustrated, they shift their thinking away from themselves and refocus on being a help to others.

Michael Rogers, a leadership speaker, shared this story on his blog about Brother Leo, a monk who died at a very old age in the year 1270:

> There is a legend that is told of a French monastery known throughout Europe for the exceptional leadership of a man known only as Brother Leo. Several monks went on a pilgrimage to visit this extraordinary leader to learn from him. Starting out on the pilgrimage, they almost immediately began to argue over who should do certain chores.
>
> On the third day of their journey, they met another monk also going to the monastery; he joined them. This monk never bickered about doing chores and did them dutifully. And

when the others would fight about which chores to do, he would simply volunteer to do them himself. On the last day of their journey, the others began to follow his example and the bickering stopped.

When the monks reached the monastery, they asked to see Brother Leo. The man who greeted them laughed. "But our brother is among you!" And he pointed to the fellow who had joined them.

Wow, what a poignant example of servant leadership.

The following chart, introduced to me by Rod Bartell, shows the five levels of leadership, which we will be discussing throughout the remainder of the book.

5 Levels of Leadership

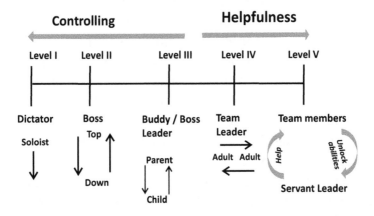

To better understand the Servant Leader at Level V, let's examine Levels I through IV.

Level I – Dictator

Level I is the classic dictator—the soloist. They exist, and no one else really matters. In business, they bark orders and do not want questions—just action. This can and does produce short-term results. In fact, it can be positive when there is urgency or danger, which includes when the safety of self and others might be at stake. From time to time, all leaders must communicate at a Level I perspective. The downside is when this becomes a dominant or even secondary response, which leads to intimidation and fear. I actually had a manager tell me that he learned the secret of motivation—to make everyone fear him equally! He actually believed that he could create teamwork and collaboration if his team feared him. WHAT?!

The best example I have heard for being an effective Level I communicator is when a trauma doctor works with a team during medical emergencies. The doctor must control the team and they must react quickly to save a patient's life. What he learned through coaching was how to move from Level I to Level II, where the team could have positive conversations following the emergency.

Our military teaches Level I leadership skills to officers because they have responsibility for men and women under command who may face life-and-death combat situations. This style of leadership worked to our country's benefit when the troops returned from World War I and worked in the assembly lines of the industrial revolution, which coincided with the growth of immigration and language barriers. During World War II, many men and women only knew Level I leaders, who took charge and accomplished much.

Today, I've coached founders of lucrative companies, entrepreneurs who started a business with passion and a right way of doing things. It was easy to lead and manage the company when it was in their garage, but became very challenging as their business grew and they had to hire more employees with almost zero training in how to manage and lead people. Therefore, they just barked orders and got short-term results.

I had dinner with a man who started a company, and in thirty years grew it to a $50 million enterprise. He ran it with an iron fist and a strong belief in yelling at vendors and subcontractors. His goal was to intimidate others, not be helpful. At the time of our meeting, he had hit a wall that was hard for him to scale. His desire was to pass on his business to the next generation and he wanted me to help him get his millennial children to lead the company the way he did—be nice to employees and brutal to everyone else. That won't work with millennial leaders or employees. Unfortunately, the Level I leader will only want to be a situational Servant Leader when it benefits them. Guess who needs to change? It's never too late. Read my next book[1] to see the results of the above Level I leader.

Level II – Top-Down Boss

Level II is when we want to be recognized as the boss. Yes, we will listen to other suggestions and ideas, but after all, we get paid the big bucks so we need to make all final decisions. Our people begin to feel more empowered because they now have a voice and potential to influence. As a result, bosses at Level II begin to motivate and recognize that building trust and respect has its place and directly impacts performance. The Level II leader-boss has a great sense of self-worth, perhaps has worked years to finally be promoted to management, and is determined not to blow it. Usually he or she toggles back and forth from Level I and II, depending on the situation.

Many times, the Level II boss has spent years under other Level II bosses, admiring how smart they seemed and always seemed to make the right choice. This created a hunger to someday be known or seen as that person of authority to make things happen and to be rewarded for results. They have a feeling of great accomplishment, and to a degree entitlement, in being selected as the general manager, global vice president, CFO, or CEO. They have a sense that, "I made it and now that I'm in the position, I should be respected." Keep in mind, not all these feelings are bad and do not necessarily arrive from an unhealthy ego. However, without growth, ego does become a reality and motives switch ever so subtly to control. Now it becomes about "me, my success, and my advancement."

The challenge for Level II leaders is that their followers seldom take initiative. They like to be told what to do and how to do it. The need for the leader-boss is to supervise. For example, you may hear from your team, "Is this right?" "What do you want me to do next?" This creates an "importance and power" mentality in the leader due to the dependency environment the leader created.

In 2001, I finally got my chance to shine. I was the owner of a franchise! I would run an organization, be respected, and have everyone marvel in amazement at my success and how I sell and instruct. So, I hired "Yes" people and made videotapes of myself doing everything right so my people could go study how their leader did things and be as successful as me. I even hired a professional videographer! I had my team come to State College so I could have a "paid crowd" and filmed myself talking about my success and how I sold millions of dollars of training.

Looking back, it was so embarrassing that I have burned all the tapes. I actually thought that all current and future sales associates would go home and watch the tapes. Can you imagine, "Hey honey, gather the kids and neighbors were going to watch another John video." Barf. I actually paid more than $20,000 to produce a recruiting tape to give to all prospective associates to show them how successful I had been. I wondered why the team was not as excited as I was—and now I think of all the smart people who took one look and ran. I have also destroyed that tape as well.

This tactic actually worked for a couple years, but I even question that now. In other words, what if I had just unleashed the talent of the team rather than dictate and guide them? Oh, they had some great ideas—but mine were always better, and in time they would understand.

The biggest challenge with the Level II leader is that we actually believe we are being helpful—that's our blind spot. We think through our ego when we think our words and actions will be helpful to others. Actually, we want to control them to do what we believe is right. This unleashes nothing. It only trains adult children to wait to be told what to think, say, or do, based on what their Level II leader believes.

Level III – Buddy/Boss or Parent/Child

The buddy/boss Level III is a trap because it sounds so wonderful! We like each other! We are actually friends. We have drinks after work. We go to baseball games and tailgate together. We are so proud of our team's successes because they act like us. One-on-one meetings serve a major purpose—so our people can ask for advice and sit at our feet. We think that our wisdom amazes them. We have a sense of connectedness.

I was coaching Stephen who was stuck at Level III. He wanted to be a teacher his whole life. Instead, he was leading an agriculture business. He saw himself as the great wise one and thought that every coaching opportunity was a teachable moment—and he expected his top team to seek out his wisdom. This created a trap. He couldn't get things done because there was always a line at his door, team members seeking his guidance and friendship.

This situation also reminds me of Tim who was leading a highly technical manufacturing process in three countries. When I first met him, he must have studied my focus, because he had all the Servant Leader lingo memorized. We took a tour of his facility; and when we finally arrived at his office, there were eight people waiting to talk to him. We went into his office and I asked him what they wanted. He said, "Oh, that's my life as a Servant Leader. Those are my 'direct reports' who have questions to ask me." What?! Well, needless to say, we had lots to discuss together about servant leadership. Today, no one knows where his office is because he empowered his team to be self-reliant and confident—and he got promoted!

Some leaders confuse Level III (buddy/boss) with Level V (the Servant Leader), but in reality, they are miles apart. The buddy/boss style falls apart when there are performance issues and corrective action is needed. During the accountability process when corrective action or directive coaching takes place, the associates wonder, *Hey, where did my buddy go? I'm not even sure if I'm invited to the tailgate tomorrow. This reprimand feels a lot like the boss is a Level I dictator leader. I wonder who he will be tomorrow—boss or buddy. I'm not sure I can trust him.*

Parent/Child – In this relationship, we actually view and treat our subordinates as children. We wish they would sit at our feet and listen to our advice that life has taught us, and then use that wisdom to be better children. The biggest problem with this mindset is that we are training subordinates to be good children— not necessarily good, productive employees. As mom or dad, we want to will fix everything, because we know best. After all, father knows best.

I had the opportunity to coach a global CEO who was doing business through a network in every region in the world. He continued to treat individuals in the network as children, which was beginning to cause some issues. To emphasize the parent/ child point I was trying to make, I started calling him "Dad." It upset him, but he got the message. We made a little progress, then he eventually retired and the organization hired a true Servant Leader—and what a difference it has made throughout the organization.

Following the parent/child style is disastrous for two reasons. The development of your team is limited to your competencies and skills which is counterproductive in helping others grow. More important, it impacts the organization's communications. For example, when you were a teenager, did you tell Mom and Dad everything? When we were parents of teenagers, did we want to know everything? Now when we apply the parent/child relationship in a business setting, we are making decisions without all the necessary information. No wonder our businesses oscillate and do not advance as we desire.

I had a client whose adult children served as members of the senior leadership team. Problem? Yes, because the owners led at a Level III, so the "leaders" never led. It took years to move them toward Level V, mainly because the parents did not want to give up perceived power. The kids loved it because there was very little accountability in the organization.

Another example. Several years ago I was asked to visit a new company to conduct a leadership assessment on their top ten leaders. My client had just bought the business. I ran a series of workshops and met with all the leaders one-on-one. What an interesting assignment! One discovery was a fear to talk to certain leaders. I heard comments like, "John, don't talk to Chuck today. He's in a bad mood, better just leave him alone." I asked, "How often does this happen?" The answer, "Oh, two or three times a week." The boss was a classic parent Level III guy.

Of course, to their surprise and alarm, I walked right into Chuck's office with a hardy "Good morning! How's it going, Chuck!" He was not mad; perhaps hung over. He had a high-strung, conscientious temperament mired in details of several problems. He had no interest in how others perceived him. This is an example and the major challenge of the parent/child Level III leadership style. People are fearful to give the parent-boss bad news. Yet, this guy is making decisions and solving problems because, hey, Dad knows best.

Paradigm Shift – Control to Helpfulness

Level IV – Team Leader

At Level IV we drive out fear. Here we work together and increase our intelligence. Have you ever felt you were working together, alone? If so you know you are not working in a Level IV team. Here we are focused on the pleasing results and desired outcome and *together* we work to achieve those results. Success and failure are felt equally among your peers. An observer might actually be challenged and not know who's the official boss. At Level IV you see the leader take full responsibility for failures and give all successes to the team.

The shift from "me" to "we" is evident in a Servant Leader's collaborative efforts. Decision making is mutually agreed upon when all the information is shared. The focus is clearly on the issue and not any one person or group. The Level IV leader treats people as adults and is always thinking about the adult-to-adult relationship. At this level, the focus on being helpful to others emerges.

In my experience, leaders in Level IV begin to push back when being coached. Especially from individuals whose driver temperaments are all about urgency and getting things done immediately. They struggle because at first they think this type of leadership style is too slow. However, if slowing down means we can go together, it has been proven we can go farther with fewer mistakes. If we buy into the adage that "People support a world they help create," we see dramatic increase in productivity and return on investment (ROI) with Level IV leaders.

It's amazing to watch a Level IV team work through a problem and arrive at a solution. All information is shared without fear. All assumptions are challenged, facts are celebrated, clear expectations are completely understood, and, if not, they clarify with each other before they go to the next step. Weaker team members either improve or are replaced and decisions are unanimous.

What happens if there is an impasse? Seldom does it happen; but when it does, there are always prearranged processes for breaking ties. Note: at Level IV it's never the leader by title who breaks the ties. For example, in our organization we have three senior leaders who are involved in making decisions. As the owner of my franchise, you may think I get veto power when solving business and people problems. No, it's our general manager who breaks all ties, and then we move on.

The greatest examples of the Level IV leadership style are in sports. Those who follow sports can quickly think of a group of individuals who came together and accomplished the impossible. Perhaps the greatest story is the 1980 US Olympic Hockey team when a group of amateur American college kids took on the best of the professional Russian team. They won! And then they went on to win the gold medal.

Although seldom does anyone get headlines for winning in business against unbelievable odds, it happens every day with Level IV work teams and leaders. Let's examine some real-world examples.

Creation of the Apple iPhone. The numerous stories, books, and movies of the team that worked on the iPhone give examples of a Level IV teamness approach. Even CEO Steve Jobs rolled up his sleeves and became just one of the team, thinking and challenging assumptions and always clarifying expectations.

Exceeding production goals. Currently I am coaching an executive in how to interact most effectively with his new work team that he inherited when he became president of a division. His senior staff informed him that he might not last six months. Their business was worst than flat-lining, declining due to outside pressures. But in two years, they have exceeded top line and operating profit expectations; and for the first time in ten years, are executing a growth plan.

How did this happen? First, by removing fear and daring the team to think together rather than working together alone. Second, he encouraged disruptive thinking to find new ways of doing business and finding new markets. In two years the mindset shifted from, "Let's hang on and hope to retire before they shut the doors," to "We are building a profitable business."

The Continental Congress was a team of young men who came together as a body of delegates and spoke and acted collectively for the people of the colony-states that later became the United States of America.[2]

The Wright Brothers. The goal of creating a flying machine drove the Wright brothers and family to work as a team to accomplish the collective goal. They covered, challenged, invested, supported, and encouraged each other to achieve the goal. Support was key. Remember, the entire scientific world was not taking them seriously the media did not really believe it was worth writing about. And even the US War Department refused to back them. In fact, one high-ranking government official questioned that even if it was a success, so what?[3] Would it really have an impact on people's lives?

The Level IV leader's major role is to consistently keep the outcome or vision in focus and to make sure everyone clearly sees and owns the current reality. Result: everyone is involved in creating actions and strategies to move successfully from the current reality to the desired outcome. Then when the action steps are taken, the team holds each other accountable to the timeframes. This focus keeps the leader's efforts on being totally helpful to others—doing whatever it takes to become the raving fan of other people's successes.

The challenge is that our egos keep creeping back into the equation and pulling us back to Level III (buddy/boss) and II (top-down) leadership. It is hard work staying at Level IV (Team Leader); there must be a continuous, conscious effort.

Level V – The Servant Leader

It takes a radical leap from Level IV to reach Level V, the Servant Leader. It takes a mindset shift from thinking, *People exist to help me accomplish my outcomes and goals* to *I exist to help people in my organization, team, family, tribe, etc. achieve their success.* Making this shift means that together we achieve our shared outcomes and goals. Our intention is to lift others up. We are not the stars; rather, we are the star makers.

The core DNA of a Servant Leader is helpfulness. Those we help are more likely to unleash their talents for the good of all. The disconnect appears when we feel we are helpful from *our* point of view and not *theirs* (Level III). We may actually think the team meeting we had on Tuesday was very helpful to the team. Wrong thought process. The Servant Leader is more interested in knowing if the meeting was helpful from the team's perspective. The Servant Leader does not ask, "How can I be helpful?" Rather, a Servant Leader is always asking for feedback. "Was the meeting helpful?" "If not, why not?" "What would be more helpful in the future?" And then follow up the responses with appropriate action.

There are times when the helpfulness of the coaching, delegation, or corrective action cannot be measured until some reasonable time has passed. Sometimes this type of interaction does not feel helpful to the person who is being coached or corrected. To receive appropriate feedback, we may have to allow time—perhaps days, months, or even years—to understand the totality of the circumstances to assess the degree of helpfulness from the other's person perspective.

What can never be challenged is the intent of the leader—was it to elevate the boss or to elevate the subordinate? Dale Carnegie crafted for the Servant Leader a great litmus test question to ask, "Am I genuinely interested in the other person's current and future success?"

The paradigm shift is in denying self. This goes against human nature. This is why I am in the *process* of becoming a Servant Leader—I need to pass certain tests under fire. When business is going great, Level V leadership seems wonderfully inspiring. The question is, what happens when business takes a turn, sales slump, quality issues are challenging, and safety records are unacceptable—now who will we choose to be?

Who Do You Choose to Be?

I was working with the BNFS Railroad outside Kansas City. Scott Hawthorne was the manager of a team of leaders who oversaw the maintenance of equipment used to fix or recondition the rails. During the assignment, I got to know Scott. He trusted me enough to allow me into his personal life, the life he had in the Army as a leader of special forces.

In Scott's basement hung his Army medals and the written citations that went with each medal. He had earned the Medal of Valor. The citation described how on one of his missions, Scott went back into a minefield to help two fallen soldiers while under fire and with landmines exploding. Scott was hit with shrapnel. In spite of being wounded himself, he applied first aid to the other soldiers; and then on his back, he carried each out of danger. That is an example of a Servant Leader at the highest level.

How many individuals have I figuratively left in the minefield to protect my own interest? And you?

Jim Collins, in his epic book *Good to Great,* wrote and made famous the "Level V leader." Most leaders I talked with really liked the concept Collins was writing about, but they never realized their need to explore being a Level V leader. In fact, that was my reaction in 2001, but I now realize I was stuck between Levels II and III. I missed it because I had flashes of Level V thinking in my mind, yet I operated at the Level II mindset (command and control) especially under pressure.

Collins wrote, "We were surprised, shocked really, to discover the type of leadership required for turning good companies into a great one. Compared to high profile leaders with big personalities who make the headlines and become celebrities, the good-to-great leaders seem to have come from Mars: self-effacing, quiet, reserved, even shy. These leaders are a paradoxical blend of personal humility and professional will."[4]

Changing the Culture

When Alan Mulally rescued the Ford Corporation, he modeled a Level V Servant Leader. In time, he changed the culture and the business results, but it took all his strength and iron-willed character to reap the rewards. What's interesting is that his focus was never about him; instead, it was always about helping others by holding himself and others accountable for results. Imagine what it must have been like to look the Ford Board of Directors in the eye and say great things are beginning to happen—knowing the company was still going to lose approximately $12.5 billion.

Mulally had to turn the culture from "me" to "we." It seems to have started when he had the dealer meeting in Detroit at Ford Field. He asked the executives from Ford in the front row to turn around and shout to the dealers, "We love you!" Hey, most business people do not talk like this to other business people! In fact, Mulally said he had them do it three times before the tone and body language matched the intent of the words.

The results at Ford are undeniable—just Google them. The story is how the leader led. One of Mulally's greatest challenges was driving out fear within his senior team. All other leaders would follow that example. He created a degree of collaboration that never existed before and then watched it accelerate throughout the organization. Today, to anyone looking back, the process seems to have gone fast—from setting expectations, to implementing strategy, to seeing rewards. However, in reality it was a process that went backward before advancing.

Here's a key take away from the Ford remake: maintain unwavering will. A final thought in illustrating the Servant Leader. Mulally demonstrated servant leadership winning across all generations not just the millennials, but the Y, X, and Baby Boomers as well.

I recently came across a simple mathematical formula that helped me further understand the power of Level V leadership and the importance of humility: the less it's about me equals the greater I become in the minds of others. That's not my intent, it just becomes reality.

Perhaps the best definition of servant leadership is to understand the major purpose of servicing others is to reach the highest level of accountability. After all, it's not about just being a nice person; no, it's about the unwavering will to achieve the desired results for the stakeholders.

So let's examine how the Servant Leader achieves the highest level of accountability at the risk of frustrating associates and challenging them at times to do what seems impossible.

Onward!

Summary

The Servant Leader is about helping others from the others' point of view. Helpfulness—not controlling—becomes the

Servant Leader's DNA. It's a mind shift from self to selflessness by embracing others. Building trust, respect, and credibility then becomes the currency of the Servant Leader. It's the fundamental shift from "me" to "we," which is easy to understand but most challenging to practice. Becoming a Servant Leader is always a process, and it will take a lifetime to master. However, the journey and the achieved milestones in choosing to become a Servant Leader is priceless—and can start today.

Key Questions

1. *How do you handle personal disappointments? Do you focus on yourself or others?*

2. *When does Level I (dictator) make sense? When does it become overbearing?*

3. *Why do you think Level II (top-down) is the most common and feels so natural to most leaders?*

4. *Have you ever made business decisions without all the information and later you were embarrassed? (Level III)*

5. *What would happen in your organization if you developed a servant leadership culture from top to bottom?*

Endnotes

1. *Servant Selling: How to Become a Trusted Advisor*, projected publication: Fall 2017.

2. Ron Chernow, *Alexander Hamilton* (New York: Penguin Press, 2004).

3. David McCullough, *The Wright Brothers* (New York, Simon & Schuster, 2016), 123.

4. Jim Collins, *Good to Great* (New York: HarperCollins, 2001).

CHAPTER 4

The Five Competencies of a Servant Leader

People with humility don't think less of themselves,
they just think about themselves less.
– Ken Blanchard and Norman Vincent Peale

Joe was the president of a multi-million-dollar division of a billion-dollar company. For most people, his division is a big organization; however, for Joe it was a small slice of the pie, though it played a strategic role in the corporation. Joe went to a Division I college and played football. He was a middle linebacker, the position on a football team that "hits" players on the other team. No surprise, then, that for every problem he faced, his answer was to figuratively hit it. As you can imagine, this created a few employee-relations issues.

After studying his personality temperament, I noticed he had the *perfect* profile for a middle linebacker and a *good* profile for a leader, with a couple of adjustments. Joe was a lot of fun to coach because he knew something was missing—he just couldn't put his finger on it. After our first full session, Joe realized he was a Level II leader. He thought a Servant Leader was to serve beers on Fridays after work. No, that might be Level III activity, but we were working on growing him into becoming genuinely interested, respectful, understanding, and even helpful to the teams.

Joe looked at me as if I had two heads when I explained the difference. He said, "John, did I sign up for marriage counseling or leadership coaching?"

I replied, "Oh, did you want me to speak to your wife?"

"NO!" he exclaimed. That would happen two years later when his company asked him to become the president of an entire division and move his family across the country.

If Joe thought he was in marriage counseling instead of leadership coaching, then my assignment to help him begin to shift from "me" to "we" gave him heartburn. In one of his assignments, he identified one of the strengths he admired in each of the people who reported directly to him, "direct reports." I then asked him to write two or three pieces of evidence for this person's strengths on a 3x5 index card. He said it was easy and even smiled and joked about how awesome his team was.

Then the heartburn. Now he had to go back over the next few weeks and share what he wrote with each direct report. You would have thought I asked him to give me his firstborn child. He had three weeks to complete the assignment—I started to get voice mail messages from him within four days. I finally called him and he shouted on the phone "JOHN, I have grown men weeping in my office and wives emailing me, thanking me for being such a great leader and motivator. I'm blown away! Who would have thought my Friday beer buddies needed affirmation?!"

Well, as you can imagine, the results were amazing! That year the team hit revenue goals and operating profit goals no one thought they had a chance to reach. All the ideas came from the teams. Joe was promoted and was moved to another state to run a major division.

Five Competencies

The five competencies that are the core of being a Servant Leader are helpfulness, understanding, respect, authentic interest, and humility. Let's examine the five competencies together.

Helpfulness. Helpfulness is not the common tag line, "What can I do to help?" That statement is too broad and comes across as disingenuous and a cop out. Think about it this way, in the last week, what was said or done to you that was not helpful? For example, I called the front desk of a well-known hotel chain to reserve a room, only to be transferred to the general reservations call center where the person who answered might have been sitting in another state or country—not helpful. A manager not watching the expenses—not helpful. Sending an email looking for data one could find on their own—not helpful.

Helpfulness is at the core and must be in our DNA as a Servant Leader. Dale Carnegie was right: honestly try to see the world, issues, and challenges from the other person's point of view. Appreciating someone else's perspective and then taking action directly or indirectly is what truly unleashes within others their ability to perform winning tasks and activities. The problem is that we are all wired to see the world through our experiences and arrive at a conclusion that our way is the *right* way instead of just *a* way. Getting in step with others is a challenge, and getting there just part way is not enough.

During my years serving as a sales manager, I made several blunders when I assumed I knew what the issues were instead of digging a little deeper. I was trained when responding to objections to get in step with others as soon as possible. What that meant was to be empathetic with their feelings and frustrations.

For example, here is one for the ages. We were calling on a company whose main product was Beano, an over-the-counter product that helps prevent gas from eating beans. We were attempting to sell a customer survey to help our client better understand how to market their product. I arrived in the morning, knowing only that we were meeting with a potential customer who may be interested in buying our customer feedback survey.

As we were driving to the appointment, I asked Bill, the salesman, to give me a quick overview of the issues we would be dealing with. Bill said the company had created a liquid process that when applied to foods would help control gas. I assumed he was talking about heartburn because at that time I was struggling from time to time with what I thought was severe heartburn. Hmmm, you can see where this story is going.

We arrived at the office and were quickly ushered into a big conference room. We were scheduled to meet with three distinguished female executives. After pleasantries, we addressed their big challenge: customers were reluctant to talk about their digestive problems due to embarrassment. I thought I could be helpful and jumped right in, saying, "Wow! I personally struggle with this problem and would be more than willing to share my own experiences; in fact, chocolate seems to drive me over the edge at times. I wake up my wife two or three times a night." I never figured out the wide-eyed stunned silence of the three female executives until four hours later driving down the road on my way home reviewing my awesome sales presentation. Yes, I laughed so hard I had to pull off the side of the road. Needless to say, that was a sale we did not close.

Assumptions, beliefs, and wrong paradigms can all lead to being unhelpful. Too often we apply our selective listening skills because of our "fast" processing skills. We say or do things that from the other person's point of view were not helpful. The attitude of helpfulness is hard work because sometimes to be helpful to others we need to deny our own current beliefs and paradigms and invert specific actions, meaning go in the opposite direction than what your gut tells you. Remember, Steve Jobs was fired when he dared to suggest that every person might have a personal computer on their desk in the 1970s.

Understanding. Understanding your team as individuals and as a whole is vital. Listening is key to understanding their strengths and weaknesses. Understanding their personalities and the way they think leads to more cohesive and creative teamwork. Understanding is more about what you don't say. It takes time to listen and learn about the people you expect to give you and your mission their full attention.

Several years ago, my wife and I decided to give a bottle of wine to our sales associates as a Christmas gift. For the most part, this was a winning idea. However, one family was upset because they do not drink alcohol. The gift showed a lack of understanding on my part. While it was a nice gesture, they were right. This faux pas could have been easily avoided and would have demonstrated real understanding and sensitivity if I had taken the time to dig a little deeper into the associate's preferences. Today we give nice door wreaths as gifts.

Respect. Again, think about the last time someone disrespected you. When I was recently in Kansas City facilitating a leadership retreat on servant leadership, we took a deep dive on this attitude of respect. The discussion centered on how people show disrespect when talking down to you or at you. Then the discussion moved to the subject: "What can a leader do to show respect?" Here are just a few ideas we wrote down on the flip chart:

- Honor the other person's time
- Support work-life balance schedules
- Be on time for meetings
- Always show good manners, especially in public, to employees and guests
- Speak with G-rated language with the intent of never offending anyone
- Always recognize and show respect to your family, especially your spouse and children, when at social or public events
- Actual respect is demonstrated when you really take the time to know what employees are about and what is important to them when working and in life

Authentic Interest. One of the keys to unlock the power in Dale Carnegie's book *How to Win Friends and Influence People* is Principle 4: Become genuinely interested in others. In fact, passed down through the folklore of Dale Carnegie is the story that he was on a radio show with Dr. Norman Vincent Peale, the minister who authored *The Power of Positive Thinking*. Dr. Peale turned to Dale and asked, "If you could only keep one of your thirty human relation principles, which one would it be?" Without a moment's hesitation Dale replied, "Become genuinely interested in others."

Choosing to be authentically interested in others is the ultimate denial of self. This requires being patient with others when we internally feel the urge to be abrupt and dismissing. It is hitting the pause button of life and just being with others in the moment. Focusing on the other person is the highest compliment you can give someone. It is without question a mindset emotional shift; skill and talent can only take you so far down this path to becoming authentically interested in others.

The challenge with establishing this competency into your mindset is time. We all have busy schedules and looming deadlines and we don't always have the time to be patient with others. Agree, that is not what I am talking about; rather, when you *do* have the time, do you use it on others or are you more interested in your agenda and desires.

A few years ago, we had a new associate join our team, Robert. He was in a class of mine and he wanted to join our team as an associate to spend time with me and learn. I was busy running an organization, being pulled in many different directions, and being authentic is not hitting the pause button at random just to spend time with Robert. I could have chosen to help him but was too tired or wanted to do something else that I perceived to be more meaningful at the time. To be honest, many times I just forgot to check in with him. Why? Because I was focused on my interests and not Robert's. No wonder Robert resigned and moved on. In his exit interview, at the heart of his flight was "John just didn't seem to care." That one is on me. He may have been the best team member I ever had, but I missed the opportunity to nurture him and be authentically interested in him.

Humility. According to the Oxford Dictionary, humility is defined as "a modest or low view of one's own importance; humbleness." This rarely talked about competency can be challenging to discuss. When was the last time you heard someone say a real strength is his or her humbleness? Almost never, in fact, humility is almost always observed or sensed. Recently while eating lunch, I received a call from an executive I had coached in the past. Like most of my coaching clients, we developed a friendship, so to hear from them from time to time is common. After hello, his next words were, "John, help!" He told me he just had received some troubling feedback. As a senior member of the leadership team at his company, he learned that most team members viewed him as arrant, cocky, and way too self-assured—that he would tell customers anything just to get business, and that it was impossible to deliver on his promises.

This perception did not occur overnight. On the contrary, it creeps into our methodologies and attitudes over time and is typically associated with success. We see it many times with big-time athletes whose success goes to their heads, along with millions of dollars. Success can be a disease that causes us to believe we are important. In business and life, it is wise to consider what is really important, and what we want others to think about us—the authentic us.

Think of what you have observed others doing to elevate their importance: name dropping, taking an "important" call in a meeting, always too busy to meet with individuals considered to be less important, quick to say certain activities are not their responsibility, being standoffish at public events, etc. These are not qualities that promote trust or even friendship. As a servant leader, your goal is to think of others as more important than yourself. The true essence of humility is to honor others, lift them up above yourself. After all, it's not about you, it's about them.

When I started my career in the Dale Carnegie business, I was not very humble. In fact, I believed I was a hotshot, because at the time, for five or six years, I was being recognized as one of the top salespeople in the world. Yes, there were times my head barely fit through the door. I remember thinking, *Boy is my manager ever lucky to have me with all the individual enrollments I've sold—he must shake his head in amazement.* It was not until years later, after my manager retired, when I was a franchise owner and was going through old sales records that I discovered my (humble) manager had sold *ten times* the number of personal enrollments in his first ten years in the business than I did. When we put on servant lenses, we understand that results are what really matter, not credit.

The question remains: how can we embrace, find, and keep humility, because if we don't, our servant leader lenses will become foggy. Here are some suggestions:

1. Always wear your servant leadership lenses; be about others above self.
2. Look for the good in people, resist the temptation to focus on the negative.
3. Make a list of the ten most embarrassing moments of your life. Review often.
4. Contract with the person whom you love the most to help keep you humble.
5. Make giving appreciation to others a habit.
6. Learn to sincerely apologize when you know you were wrong, and for how you may have made others feel unintentionally.
7. Give credit to others sincerely when you are experiencing success.
8. Accept complete responsibility for all failings.
9. Always ask yourself, *What would a servant do in this situation?*
10. Be a giver—always give more than you think you can afford, and then be inspired by the blessing.

This Servant Leadership competency of humility is the hardest to work on. To accept the reality of a continuous intentional effort to be humble is not easy because it is natural to want to feel important and focus on self. On the other hand, there is no greater joy to be discovered than in helping others feel important.

These five competencies are the foundation of a Servant Leader's mindset and lifestyle. It takes intentionality to be successful and to realize the importance of each five. Most executives I work with have three of the five as strengths, there are two challenged areas, and typically one of the five is a blind spot. In fact, they sometimes think the blind spot is a strength because they either do not see the relevancy nor understand the depth of the competency required to be a Servant Leader.

I was working with an executive who believed "understanding" was a strength because, per him, how could he not be? Blind spot. He listed his best friend as someone to interview as part of the coaching process in developing his feedback team. His best friend said, "I'm always embarrassed when he introduces me as his best friend, because if he thinks I'm his best friend, what a shallow life he must be leading."

Becoming a Servant Leader means recognizing that these five competencies need thought, planning, evaluation, adjustment, and coaching. Do not just grab the surface value of these important foundation components. I dare you to go deep and really challenge yourself on a regular basis, because it doesn't take much to fall off the tracks. Remember, life is busy and messy, so recalibrate often.

Onward!

Summary

Helpfulness is the cornerstone of a Servant Leader. Flowing from being helpful is understanding, respect, and showing an authentic interest in others. Finally personal humility is the pathway of becoming a servant leader. If you choose to live focusing on the five competencies, it is almost impossible to be self-centered and self-focused—and very possible to be successful in life and business.

Key Questions

1. *From an emotional perspective, based on what you think and feel, how much do you really care about others?*

2. *What new actions might you take when you emotionally embrace the idea of being helpful to others from their perspective?*

3. *What questions could you ask someone to enhance your ability to truly understand their situation? Are you listening to what is not being said as well as the answer?*

4. *How have you shown a lack of respect to others in the past week? What were the consequences you suffered as a leader?*

5. *What do you do every day to show an authentic interest in others?*

CHAPTER 5

Mindset Shift from "Me" to "We"

Project authenticity and vulnerability, be present, be accepting, and see your role as being useful, as being the servant. –James A. Autry, Practicing Servant Leadership

Mark just finished a staff meeting with his new team. He had recently been promoted to head a global division and now occupied the corner office. I have been coaching Mark for the past six years, and we have developed a very positive business relationship—high trust and respectful. After Mark had ushered the last person out of the conference room and we returned to the big corner office, he looked around outside his door to be sure no one was looking for him, then shut the door, and walked over to his desk.

I was still admiring the view when Mark said, "John, now what am I to supposed to do? I spent my life working to get here. I've become an expert in the industry, finally got the promotion, and now I have nothing to do. What I love to do and what I was and am really good at doing, I no longer do because I have high-level staff and talented individuals to do it all."

After we had a good laugh, we turned to the next chapter of servant leadership. In that chapter, it's no longer about Mark, it's totally about others and building his team and individual competencies—and then being more strategic in growing his division for long-term sustainable growth. True we had been talking about servant leadership for six years and no one I coached has had more passion to serve than Mark, but on that cold November morning looking out from the corner office, Mark understood the concept of moving on from "me" to "we" more deeply. And after three years, Mark's division is now the cash cow of the organization. I wonder what his next move will be, no doubt one more step up—stay tuned.

Me or We?

Desert Pete lived in the Mojave Desert in Arizona and was a well-known guide. One day a group wanted to strike out on their own and asked him for a day's walk. Pete described a great trail with plenty of water, but with one small challenge. Approximately fifteen miles into the walk was a drinking well with a pump. When primed correctly, it would produce an unlimited amount of water for the entire group—important when walking in the desert. The key words are "when primed." Pete explained that two feet away from the well under a well-marked rock was a canteen full of fresh water to prime the pump. To do that, about one-third of the water has to be dumped into the well and then the handle pumped 10-12 times to start the process, then the remainder of the water from the canteen had to be dumped in to finish the priming process. Then pump and pump the well not stopping for three to four minutes—then the well would produce a tremendous amount of water with just a little bit of pressure. Desert Pete then reminded the group that after they had their fill of water, they must refill the canteen and place it under the rock for the next group.

I wonder how many people arrive at the well being very thirsty and take a swig first—running the risk of not being able to prime the pump for others? How hard is it for people to make the shift from focusing on "me" to "we"?

For my daughter Jackie's 18th birthday, my wife Colleen and I decided to take her to Las Vegas to see a Celine Dion concert. She was excited beyond belief. This trip was six months in the planning—flight and hotel reservations were made and our entire trip was planned around this event. We were playing Celine CDs, and Jackie would sing along. As the day approached, final reservations were made at restaurants and other activities as well. We arrived in Vegas, had an awesome day and night out, then woke the morning of the concert with tremendous anticipation. We relaxed by the pool, dressed, and went for an early dinner. Finally it was time to walk to Caesars Palace to the concert. When we arrived at the ticket office, we saw the sign: CONCERT CANCELED due to Celine's sore throat.

Trust me there was no "WE" mindset among us at that moment. Each of us were equally frustrated, mad, upset, and angry. We were each thinking, *How dare this person get sick on my night—the night I planned for months and spent a lot of money to be here! What an inconvenience for me!*

What would have been the servant "we" mindset? Saying sincerely, "I hope it's not serious and that she is resting well. Did she receive medical help? Here is a note to send her wishing her well. I hope she doesn't hurry back and endanger her vocal cords. Tell her not to worry, we will reschedule when she is feeling better."

Anyone can be considerate about others when it's convenient, but what about when it's not? The mind shift from "me" to "we" is not only when things are going good or when it's convenient; rather, it's an intentionally ingrained DNA response, regardless of the circumstances. That is why it's a process, not an event.

The following attitudes and emotions represent the "me" mindset—being focused on yourself, not others:

- Frustration
- Anger
- Fear of speaking in front of groups
- Choosing not to coach
- Choosing not to delegate
- Choosing not to raise the bar
- Choosing not to take corrective action

- Criticizing, condemning, or complaining
- Not showing appreciation
- Not being an encourager
- Choosing not to give feedback
- Not holding others accountable
- Not listening
- Not remembering names
- Losing emotional control

Choosing with intention and purpose the opposite of these attitudes and emotions is shifting to the "we" mindset. A deeper dive takes us to understanding the difference between personal victim thinking and personal ownership thinking.

Victim Thinking Versus Personal Ownership Thinking

The mindset shift from victim thinking to ownership thinking is shown in the following chart. Note: There must be an emotional shift as well as a thinking shift.

Victim thinking takes no effort—it's most people's default position. When I choose to be on my "A" game and purposefully shift my mindset to take personal ownership, I realize it's a choice that must be made daily. It reminds me of the humorous yet true-to-life Servant Leader's daily prayer:

Dear Lord, so far today, I've done all right. I haven't gossiped, and I haven't lost my temper. I haven't been grumpy, nasty, or selfish, and I'm glad of all that! But in a few minutes, Lord, I'm going to get out of bed, and from then on, I'm probably going to need a lot of help. Thank you! Amen.

In coaching executives away from victim thinking, I've discovered that they must develop a renewed vision of who they choose to become. They can build personal ownership thinking into the exciting future of who they want to become. The most challenging people to coach are leaders of family-owned businesses, especially dealing with second and third generations. Not shifting a victim mindset appropriately is one of the reasons why second and third generation businesses fail at an alarming rate. The challenge I have faced is when victim thinking is embedded in past family history. Some family-run business executives get bogged down in past perceived injustices.

	Victim	Ownership
View of Life	- Others get all the breaks. - Jealous of others' accomplishments, possessions, and positions. - Life is unfair while waiting for others to recognize my talents.	- Make their own breaks. - Delights in others' successes. - Believes that life is neither fair nor unfair, making their own breaks.
View of Work	- People are promoted and given opportunities due to politics. - Other people and circumstances contribute to any poor performance on their part. - Believe they're right and smart; other people just don't get them. - Look for the easy methods and ways out of trouble.	- Believe they are 100% responsible for career path. - Proactive in building relationships. - Believe they can intentionally make things happen. - Sees and owns mistakes; understands, corrects, and learns from mistakes. - Focuses on results, not pleasing or easier methods.
Their Future	- Future is limited due to circumstances. - Unsatisfied with current state and always look back to individuals who "hurt" them.	- See unlimited possibilities in their future. - Great satisfaction of current state and are always thankful to those who helped, positively or negatively.
Approaches to Mistakes	- Blame game—not my fault. - Throws others under the bus—no support for others. - Looks to proactively find others' mistakes to make themselves look good.	- Take responsibility for their part of the mistake and learn from it. - When possible choose to cover for others. - Dealing with mistakes is to be helpful so others can get desired results.

Family Matters

In one organization I was working with, the family members were conflicted and arguing about company-won trips based on performance. They never even considered what made sense for the business, they based their decisions on victim thinking, "She's always been the favorite," etc. Personal ownership thinking in making decisions advanced the company and stopped the practice of doling out company trips like Christmas gifts.

Another CEO I was working with had a hard time making decisions because of perceived negative feelings toward him by his brothers and sisters. Another example of victim thinking is the "woe is me" syndrome. Taking on the ownership mindset, we can put personal concerns aside and make decisions on behalf of winning in the market and the success of the company that supports the families of those who come to work each morning.

My father taught me a lesson on taking personal ownership when I was in grade school. Dad had me raise two baby pigs. After I got off the bus from school each day, I had to change from my school clothes into a pair of jeans and work boots and it was my responsibility to walk about a mile to feed my smelly pigs. I was told that after ninety days we would sell the pigs at the farmer's market. Pigs were sold by the pound, so the fatter the pigs, the more money I would have for Christmas and to deposit into my savings account. The first year went well and when we sold my pigs at the market, I received a check for $74.70. I thought I was the richest guy in the world. All the effort paid off—even though I had to walk a few times in the wind, rain, and cold in November afternoons. My grandmother was so excited and proud to take me to the bank and make that deposit into my savings account; at 1.5 percent interest, she showed me how much money I would make without working. The interest was like an extra payday for those who work hard.

Well, the next year did not go so well. The victim inside voice arrived with a year of experience and increased wisdom. After all, not feeding the pigs a couple of times would not hurt—after all, they were just pigs. Then when it rained, well maybe they would survive without being fed, and other days I just had more interesting things to do. In fact, it was not my fault, I told my younger brother Jimmy to feed the pigs, and I would give him a quarter. Well, he got distracted and didn't always follow through, so it was Jimmy's fault that when we sold the pigs my check was only for $21.06.

Oh, you can be sure my dad and I had a conversation—and he bought none of my excuses. However, it was my conversation with my grandmother, when I had no money to deposit into my bank account, that I will never forget—just the look on her face taught me an early lesson about personal ownership and responsibility.

Taking personal ownership for myself was reinforced in high school in the 10th grade. I was on the junior varsity wrestling team, feeling badly that I could not make the varsity team. During practice on one dreary day in January, we were assigned to do twenty-five push-ups. Because I was feeling sorry for myself and thinking only how miserable I was in the moment, I only did twelve push-ups because who cared and who would know. Well, Coach Karl Reisner noticed and cared. He casually walked by and said in a voice only I could hear, "Rodgers, how am I going to make you a national prep school champion if you won't even take responsibility to do twenty-five push-ups?" Then he walked on.

That one question shifted me from the miserable moment to an exciting possible future and the realization that I had to take personal ownership of my future—it would never be handed to me. That question shifted my mindset, and the following March I became a National Prep All-American by placing third place at the national tournament held each year at Leigh University.

My business coach, Kevin Crone in Toronto, Canada, challenged my thinking by saying that my business was not about my accomplishments and awards, rather it was about my customers. He pointed me in a new direction, and soon I was asking myself, *In what ways can I help my customers be more*

successful...I want to be 100 percent focused on them winning.
Then I started organizing a team not to benefit me and my
personal gains, but rather organizing a team that could serve our
customers by celebrating their wins. Then we celebrated
individual team member's successes in better serving customers
and achieving their personal successes. Now I can I enjoy the
sense of satisfaction by helping others win in life and business.
Shifting from "me" to "we."

Summary

We have to work through the process of shifting our paradigms
to see through new lenses, to see what seems impossible and
make it possible. The Servant Leader strives to maintain the
mindset of growth, ownership, and abundance. The opposite
mindset is fixed on victimhood and scarcity. The shift from
victim to ownership is vital—and another reason why becoming
a Servant Leader is a process.

Key Questions

1. *What causes you to stay in the "me" mindset?*

2. *What negative consequences do you experience by staying in
    the "me" mindset?*

3. *What has worked for you in the past to shift your mindset
    from "me" to "we"?*

4. *How would your personal relationships change if you were
    successful in shifting from "me" to "we"?*

5. *How does understanding the phrase, "The less it is about me
    equals the greater I become in the minds of others" govern
    your ego?*

CHAPTER 6

Personal Vision

Forget yourself by becoming interested in others. Do every day a good deed that will put a smile of joy on someone's face.
– Dale Carnegie

I was driving on route 80 heading west mid-afternoon when my cell phone rings. I see it's Mac, a man I'm coaching. Mac works for a division of a large food store chain; his role is to build new, large grocery stores, design, build, stock, hire, train, and introduce the store employees to the new general manager and then move on to his next assignment. When his sponsor contacted me, the coaching project was rather simple, Mac needed to work on his interpersonal relational skills. The sponsor told me that Mac was very talented, he knew every department in the business and how it needed to be set up and run to maximize profits. The problem was that he is so hard on people that they actually cheer when he moves on to his next assignment. So you get the full picture of how intimidating Mac could be, he is 6'5" and weighs 280 pounds.

I answered my cell phone and barely said good afternoon when Mac starts talking—and by his tone, he was not happy. "John, don't you even try to talk me out of this one because tomorrow afternoon when my peer arrives from corporate, I'm going to shut my door, grab him by the neck, and throw him up against the wall. Then I'm going to get in his face and tell him that if he ever gives advice to my meat manager again that violates code to the extent that if an inspector would walk through my store and see what you ordered my manager to do, they would lock our doors. You blankety blank blank!"

I simply responded with a statement and a question, "Wow, I get why you're angry, and I know how the old and present Mac will react...you made that quite clear. My question is, how will the guy, the leader you desire to become, how would he choose to respond?"

In our coaching sessions, we had been spending a lot of time analyzing who he was and is, and we were beginning to paint a different picture of who he wanted to become. He envisioned not being pigeon-holed into his current role working at the local store level. He could see a promotion to the parent company and impacting the $6 billion operation. Personally, he wanted to connect better with his wife and nephews.

The good news is that Mac chose to respond to his peer with a futuristic mindset which resulted in creating a win-win resolution. Oh yes, corrective action and peer coaching took place, but Mac did it in a way that was helpful toward his peer's knowledge of the situation; the conversation was not negative or degrading, which may have stunted his development. Mac told me later that this was a peer he had worked with for five years without ever communicating, yet within two weeks the peer called him no less than five times asking for advice in other stores.

Realize your power to choose who you want to become—and then get busy being that person. No, you are right, I can't physically place you in your future, but you can move yourself in thought. What would happen today if you began to think as if you were, and not as you currently are?

Your personal vision should always be adjusting to life's lessons, experiences, and circumstances. Once you get it, enjoy it for the moment—but what you will learn tomorrow, next week, next month, and next year should always force an adjustment. If not, all those thoughts that you see and hear causes mental weariness and the clear vision you had loses focus. Remember, the sharper your picture of who you are becoming, the easier and more targeted your decisions are today.

Current and Future Reality

Your vision is also important so that you can create structural tension between who you want to become and the current reality of who you are. This tension will create clear pathways and logical actions to take to move yourself from your current reality to your desired state. For one young female executive I was working with, this tension made her realize she needed to check herself into rehab. Why? Because the person she desired to become kept falling short due to an addiction to alcohol. Good for her! She took action so she could get busy becoming the person in her dreams. She now has been alcohol free for over a year, lost 60 pounds, and is not just feeling and looking better—she is able to make better life decisions based on the person she is desiring to become.

My son Sam had a vision at age 14. He was so excited he wrote it down and had me sign it. Then he transformed himself for the next five years until he arrived at Syracuse University on a full football scholarship.

> If I Sam Rodgers receives a full four (4) year scholarship to College you John Rodgers will buy me a car from the price range of twenty five thousand (25,000) to thirty thousand (30,000). I will receive this car the beginning of my sophomore year.
>
> x _____
> x _____ February 12, 2006

What did vision do for Sam? It put him on a five-year path to accomplishing his goal. His vision ended his daily unhealthy habits such as: drinking soda, eating candy, cookies, and sweets, no more McDonald Big Mac meals, milk shakes, and other foods kids love. Instead, he became serious about nutrition. He began to take seriously the prospect of developing his new-found love of long-snapping; the long snapper hikes the ball to a holder or punter during extra points, field goals or punts. After warm-ups, Sam would snap balls between 50-100 times every day. He started working out and running in the morning, lifting twice a day just because he could—and he knew most of his competition were still in bed. Most people don't realize how much effort it takes to live out a vision. Sam's hard work behind the scenes earned him success. The actions that the vision instills in people is just awesome.

In the summer before Sam's sophomore year, we took a father-son trip to the Baseball Hall of Fame in Cooperstown, New York—in his new car. I remember challenging him, "So what's next now? Who will you get busy becoming?" He said, "Well, I earned the starting positions as a freshman, so I want to finish my last three years well, and have an opportunity to play professional football, but the challenge is that there are not real awards for snapping." While Sam was playing football at Syracuse 2011-2014 no one was awarding All-American status to Long Snappers. "Ok," I challenged, "so what can you do?" And for the next two hours Sam talked about what he could accomplish— who he could choose to become in the next three years that would influence his behavior and aspirations following graduation and for the rest of his life.

The following is what happened to him, in no particular order:

- First team Academic All-American Team
- Elected team captain his senior year by his teammates
- Chosen to join the All-States Good Hands Team
- Syracuse Remembrance Scholar
- Team member of All Big East and ACC Academic teams
- Two-years as president of the Fellowship of Christian Athletes

You can imagine the wise choices Sam made to bring about these accomplishments. Now he is in law school—can you guess what our vision conversations are about?

The power of vision drives actions and attitudes that allows people to create a future exciting picture that can win in life and business—if they take the time to imagine their vision.

The Purpose of Vision

The driving reason Servant Leaders work hard at developing and updating their vision is to be of better service to others. When working with others, it's always important to challenge them to think in terms of who they want to become. This remains the most powerful tool in coaching, because when we get other people focused on who they want to become, their imaginations and energies take over. Then they create new ways of thinking, working, and playing that benefit them. Nothing is more motivating for people than taking action or making changes that will help them get closer to whom they want to become.

Another key understanding about vision and building a personal vision is that it must be 360 degrees in nature. Your professional vision is only one small aspect of your life, although it happens to drive a lot of meaning and actually creates the means for other life focuses. Consequently, you should have a future vision as to who you want to become in all aspects of life. Paul Batz and Tim Schmidt wrote a book entitled *What Really Works: Blending the Seven Fs for the Life You Imagine* in which they talk about blending the seven Fs—Faith, Family, Finances, Fitness, Friends, Fun, Future. Two really neat thoughts from the book: first, the blending idea creates the most success; and second, work is not part of the seven Fs, which ties into other learnings—that work is not who we are, work is only what we do.

Their book gave me two interesting perspectives on the work-life balance of a Servant Leader. Obviously the seven Fs, but more importantly was the blending of the seven Fs, which has really helped me in coaching executives in building a well-rounded vision. The following is my take on the seven Fs from a Servant Leader's paradigm.

Faith. Servant Leaders are grounded. They have an internal compass, a true north. I have seen this in leaders with a variety of faiths. In fact, one of the most interesting people I coached was a self-proclaimed atheist. I always enjoy and learn from others when they think different from the way I think or believe. Faith talk makes a lot of folks nervous; it can be polarizing because most people of faith have strongly held opinions. My encouragement is for you to intentionally grow in your faith because it causes a sense balance when you are aligned with who you are as a leader in life and work.

To the contrary, I have met individuals who lack a faith walk or ignore faith, and there is always something missing in their character. It appears they are always searching. The older we get the more established we become in our ways and beliefs. However, as we experience life through different lenses, especially our lenses of faith, we encounter things in life that make no sense, yet we know we can endure; challenges arise that catch us off-guard, yet we know it will work out; and associates and peers look to us for answers when there aren't easy answers. When an associate dies suddenly, a car accident, a family crisis, someone has cancer—at these times, money, position, and influence are of little significance. It's moments like these when a faith walk provides stability.

Family. Servant Leaders refine their servant attitudes at home. At home is the most challenging because we are dealing with people we love the most. If this is not the case, then it's likely the reflection of the most broken and hurtful relationship in our lives. How to serve as a spouse, parent, and child takes on new meanings as we age.

When I think of family, I tend to think of my immediate family: children, spouse, and extended family of parents and brothers and sisters, etc. However, I realize others might have a different perspective of family due to life's circumstances.

Therefore, I do not intend to limit the definition of family to just traditional thinking but open up to embrace all definitions that engage in loving, caring relationships that are committed to each other through thick and thin.

I also realize that often we encounter broken family relationships; some hurts are so deep and seem almost unforgiving. With my servant lenses, I encourage all broken relationships to seek healing; life is too short, and if we remember as a servant that it's not about us, many times we can find the opportunity to seek reconciliation.

Finances. Only 18 percent of US workers say they are very confident of having enough money to live comfortably during their retirement years, per the Employee Benefit Research Institute. If true, what are the 82 percent of people doing every day who aren't confident of the future? This isn't addressing only savings, it also reflects our attitude toward earnings and spending. Point being, it's hard to maximize the other Fs without budgeted dollars. You value what you spend money on and for. Obviously, major expenses are your house, cars, and college education for your children. Financial acumen is important in establishing work-life balance because I know of no other factor that can cause the most amount of stress in a family. The other factor very little attention is given to is your tolerance for risk. This must be agreed upon with your spouse and measured to help you make wiser choices toward paying off debt or building savings.

In Og Mandino's book *University of Success,* he put together the thinking of some of the best motivational writers of the 20th century. One lesson that Mandino shared was from George S. Clason's most famous story, "The Richest Man in Babylon," where the heart of the story is the commitment to save—never to spend 10 percent of your earnings. This simple principle will ensure that you are part of the 18 percent who will retire financially independent, regardless of your current income.

Fitness. Fitness means maintaining a positive energy throughout your day and week. This gives you the opportunity to finish well. Do you look like you could still run a 40-yard dash in under 10 seconds? More importantly, does your physical energy parallel your mental energy? With the natural circumstances of aging aside, what are you doing intentionally to sustain stamina during the work day and drive home safely? Your choice of exercise can vary; and the older you get, most experts suggest some form of cross-training to use all muscle groups so not to overexert one body area.

Be creative; make life interesting by thinking about what exercise you can do with family and friends. Blending the seven Fs is critical per author and coach Paul Batz. My current exercise choices are walking, swimming, and biking. All three of these give me time to think about planning and strategy purposes in my life and work.

A whole new area is being studied in the business world—nutrition. Oh, this is not new to the sports world, but until recently not a lot of studies were published about eating and drinking your way to business success. It makes total sense; after all, athletes think about what they put into their bodies for days before competition—why not business professionals. For example, you have a major sales presentation in two days and you want to be performing at optimum mental speed during the meeting. So, are you fueling your body with jet fuel or with Debbie's powdered donuts with a quart of chocolate milk?

Friends. Let's first look at a factual definition of a friend. The dictionary says a friend is a person whom one knows and with whom one has a bond of mutual affection, typically exclusive of sexual or family relations.

Allow me to expand—a friend is a person whom you trust, respect, and enjoy being with. A friend is a person who understands that at times you need an ear, not advice; someone with whom you can be transparent and real. A friend is a person who will hold you accountable to living out your values and confronts you in a gentle way when you don't.

Friendship relationships take work—they don't just happen. Acquaintances, on the other hand, just happen: two people meet, have fun, agree on most topics, laugh together, then go their separate ways until they somehow meet again.

Michael W. Smith wrote a song about friendship:

> *And friends are friends forever*
> *If the Lord's the Lord of them*
> *And a friend will not say never*
> *'Cause the welcome will not end*
> *Though it's hard to let you go*
> *In the Father's hands we know*
> *That a lifetime's not too long*
> *To live as friends.*

Future. It is important to see the future and then think and act as if it's already a reality. I had the privilege of facilitating a Dale Carnegie class just for fathers who had lost their jobs and who were experiencing challenging life circumstances. In the first session, we were working on writing a personal vision and seeing the exciting future picture of who they wanted to become in three to six months.

In the front row of the class was Bob. He looked at me with a blank stare through the entire process. During the break, he came up to me and said, "John, I am not sure if I can see dinner tonight let alone tomorrow. So six months from now seems impossible." After class I sat down with him and learned the following. After Bob had lost his job, he could not visit his three children who now lived with his ex-wife 30 miles away. The reason: he had no car.

After our discussion, we realized that his six-month goal was to get a car. In fact, he had scoped out a 1978 Cadillac at a used car dealership for $3800.00. Why a Cadillac for a man who had no job and no car? It had enough space in the backseat for three car seats and he felt his three kids would be safe while riding in it. It was simple to create the exciting vision of Bob purchasing a 1978 Cadillac. If he could buy the car that meant he had a job to purchase the car, pay child support, and become the dad he desired to be.

Almost a year later while having dinner with my family at a Subway, we ran into Bob. After exchanging pleasantries Bob asked me to follow him—he had something to show me. So we walked out into the parking lot, down two rows and the third car was a 1978 Blue Cadillac, freshly washed, and looking good. Bob looked at me and said with a smile and tears running down his cheeks "John, now you know the answers to your questions... I got a job, I'm current on my child support payments, and I am becoming the father I desire to be."

To the other extreme, I was talking with another man who was describing a future that I was struggling to get my arms around. He saw his business, his trust funds, his charity organization, and his great grandchildren making a difference in a world that was radically changed from anything I was familiar with at present. I finally stopped him and asked, "I'm confused with what you are describing, help me see." Then he cleared the air, "Oh, John I'm painting a picture around the year 2080." Hmmm! He was not a quack; in fact, his net worth was north of a billion dollars.

Seeing the future and always trying to expand it allows you to make better, clearer decisions today that will add to your satisfaction of living and perhaps your bank account tomorrow. Not seeing the future is like driving in fog. Seeing the future... ahhh, the fog has lifted and you can see far down the road, which influences your peace of mind as you drive forward. So it is with seeing your future.

Fun. Fun is the sheer pleasure of experiencing joy. Fun is laughing with friends at life's funny twists and turns, finding contentment with a hobby or activity, and sharing your joy with friends and family. When was the last time you laughed uncontrollably, anticipated going to a special event, dreamed of going on a vacation, attended or participated in a game?

What part of your job is fun? The work itself? The people? The sense of fulfillment? Using your talents and skills? As you approach retirement, when money is no longer the motivator, the enjoyment of the work and the interaction with others is fun. Winning in life and business by helping others is not just for personal gain—it's for the fun and joy of giving.

A challenge I have when coaching is working on developing a personal vision for and with others. For some people, it is really hard to imagine a future that seems unattainable or farfetched. The key is not to force it; after time, they settle into the idea and we go slowly until they embrace it. In fact, in my coaching sessions, there is no reason to move to the next step until they see their vision and own it. This is what motivates people to change behavior. The power of influencing yourself—changing a belief or paradigm to impact how you think and feel.

Building Vision

Ok, now let's look at how to build vision:

- What do you daydream about? Who are you helping, what are you doing, how are you perceived and being appreciated, why are you excited and have an inner glow of happiness?
- Think in positive, powerful descriptive words.
- Think big: make everything 3x (times) greater. 3x the impact, 3x the promotion, 3x the salary, 3x the house you are building or moving into, 3x the sales goal.
- Talk to others: bosses, co-workers, family, friends, and pastors.
- Make it about others: Who else is benefiting from your efforts, how are others being rewarded or winning due to your actions?
- The acid test: When you wake up in the morning and are reminded about your vision, it should put fire in your belly.

In a nutshell, vision is a powerful, positive, future exciting picture in your mind's eye. With some executives I've coached, to dramatize my point I had them draw me a picture of their future state. However, the best analogy is in thinking about completing a jigsaw puzzle. Let's examine the steps: take all the pieces out of the box, turn them right side up, hide the box, begin. You say, "What?! Hide the box? No, the picture on the front of the box guides me." Hmmm, exactly.

The analogy of the picture on the front of the box is like your vision—it guides you, it helps you make sense of all the pieces on the table. The individual pieces on the table represent all the talents, skills, and decisions you need to make to complete the full picture. Your picture or vision gives you confidence in all your decision making. Then you want to make sure your vision is always as crystal clear as possible; so make a commitment to continually refine and tweak your exciting future picture—then watch the impact it has on your decision making.

Summary

The absolute power of seeing our future reality and then begin to act as if… "what 'could be' and 'should be' regardless of what is" a powerful definition of vision I learned from Andy Stanley in his book *Visioneering: God's Blueprint for Developing and Maintaining Personal Vision*. Continually refocus and expand your vision in every area of life; this is a fundamental trait of a Servant Leader.

Key Questions

1. *Do you have a powerful, exciting personal vision or picture of the person you desire to become?*

2. *Do you work on further developing or refining your vision daily, weekly, monthly?*

3. *When you are working with individuals on your team, how often do you review and or help build their visions?*

4. *Do you understand the most powerful tool you have as a leader in coaching your associates is helping them to build their vision? If not, what is your plan of action to use this tool?*

5. *Do you get it? A vision is just a vision until you put on your Servant Leader lenses, then everything changes for you and others.*

CHAPTER 7

Achieving Breakthrough Results

If you want to conquer fear, don't think about yourself.
Try to help others, and your fears will vanish.
– Dale Carnegie

The following is a candidly honest story I came across in my reading that proves this chapter's point:

Four People

This is a story about four people named Everybody, Somebody, Anybody, and Nobody.

There was an important job to be done and Everybody was asked to do it. Everybody was sure Somebody would do it. Anybody could have done it, but Nobody did it. Somebody got angry about that, because it was Everybody's job. Everybody thought Anybody could do it, but Nobody realized that Everybody wouldn't do it. It ended up that Everybody blamed Somebody when Nobody did what Anybody could have done. –Author Unknown

Achieving servant leadership accountability is at the heart of this chapter. Level V leaders do not play the blame game; however, before we dive into how Servant Leaders hold themselves and others accountable, we need to understand the fundamentals of developing people. Note: the development and growth of people is the number 1 priority of the Servant Leader.

Let's together unpack the process.

Flying home from Minnesota in 1996, at about 30,000 feet I was looking out the window thinking about the most absurd idea I heard from a speaker from Great Brittan who was challenging us in breakthrough thinking. As I was reviewing my notes, I had no idea I was about to experience one of those watershed moments of life that turned my thoughts from frustration and despair to fascination and motivation—and *Please land the plane I have some calls to make!* A simple thought changed my life forever.

Peter Naylor, the speaker, was talking to a sales audience and asked us if we had an idea about how much income we would earn in the next year. I quickly calculated about $80,000. Then he said, "I know as sales people you probably have a couple of deals that if the stars align just right, you might earn what?" Hmmm, again I grabbed my pen did some quick calculations. I thought, *Wow, if those deals DO happen, I'll make about $95,000! That would be an amazing year and almost to my goal of earning $100,000.* Then Peter went on to say that the new calculation of $95,000 was nothing more than a stretch goal. Then he asked, "Do you want to know what a breakthrough goal would be?" My pen in hand, I was ready…thinking to myself I was about to hear the answer of how I would achieve my goal of earning $100,000 before my 40th birthday.

Then he shocked me with his next challenge. He said go back to your original earned income projection ($80,000) and multiply it by 3. Being quick at math, *Okay, that would be $240,000.* "If you achieve that," Peter said, "you have had a breakthrough." *WHAT?! He doesn't understand the challenges we have, I have, the markets have, I got a wife, kids…what a waste of time thinking about that number.* In a daze I wrote down what I heard next, thankfully, because flying at 30,000 feet I read the following: "So that shocks you and you think it seems impossible, This is good, because when you achieve it, you will know it was truly a breakthrough." Then I read the keywords that changed my mindset and life: "So in order to achieve that breakthrough, how will you need to think, work, and play differently?"

It has been said many times before that being an effective leader is taking people where they would not go by themselves. As a Level V Servant Leader, I dare you to have your team, or people around you, experience breakthrough results. In other words, have your team see a task or achievement that seems impossible, but with your coaching and helpfulness they make the impossible possible. There is no greater thrill on Earth—for them and you.

A major challenge many executives face is holding themselves and others accountable to achieving results. In most cases, where the most tension is felt is in larger organizations where revenue and profit goals are passed down and always seem to be increasing. I heard the frustration and some executives throw up their hands and shout, "How do you squeeze water out of a rock?!" The pressure is to pass on the tension by placing unreasonable goals on others.

Servant Leaders resist that temptation and shift their mindset from a fixed to a growth perspective. This does not always guarantee success, but always guarantees a better opportunity to achieve the seemingly impossible.

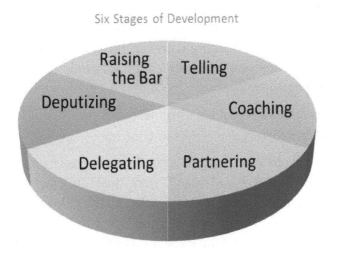

The 6-Stage Process of Development, taken from *Leadership Alignment Index* by Rod Bartell.

Stage 1 – Communicating or Telling

Operating from this stage is the leader's ability to communicate what is in his head so that it comes out his or her mouth in meaningful words that are organized to connect so that others understand, and more importantly, can take the right action to produce the right results. Here we not only need to *tell* but also *do* in a way that creates a lasting impression.

The skill in telling a story or painting a picture through the spoken word is a talent that can be developed with practice and coaching. The following are a few guidelines:

1. Think from the other person's point of view. In other words, if you were your own audience, what would you need to hear or understand to make sense of the verbal instructions?

2. Focus more time on how you look and act while speaking. Use gestures and animation to help create pictures and drive home analogies.

3. Always think and communicate from the mindset of "What's in it for them" (WIIFT). Talk about *their* benefits not yours or the company's.

A great human performance tool is three-way communication. This I learned while working with several organizations in the nuclear field. Three-way communication is as follows:

- Tell them
- Have them repeat what you just said
- Either correct and repeat or confirm

Beyond the obvious speaking skills, the most challenging skill is actually listening. We will spend more time on listening skills when we discuss the coaching stage next, but the following story is a good example. There were two college roommates from a mid-Western university. One student was a farmer from Iowa and the other student grew up in New York City in the Upper East Side neighborhood of Manhattan. During spring break, the roommate from New York invited his Iowa farmer roommate to visit New York with him. The first morning they woke up and were walking down Broadway looking and listening to all the sounds of the city. Suddenly the Iowa farm boy said, "Hey, I hear crickets." "No way," exclaimed his roommate, "we're in New York City!" Well, the farm boy walked over to a small shrub and gently moved a branch to the side and there about calf-high, sure enough there on a stem was a cricket chirping as loudly as could be.

They both had a laugh and moved on. Then within two minutes, two uniformed guards were unloading bags from a Brinks armored truck and delivering them to a bank when one of the guards tripped and spilled a bag of coins onto the street. Everyone within a half city block stopped and turned to look at the sound of coins hitting the pavement.

The farm boy from Iowa looked at his friend and said, "Isn't it interesting nobody can hear my crickets, but everyone is in tune with money." The point of the story is that as leaders we must be tuned in to the concerns and successes of others.

Stage 2 – Coaching

Coaching is the stage that most leaders fly by without realizing how important it is. Perhaps because they themselves are unclear or they assume others know and understand and even have perfected an activity, skill, or task and only need to be reminded. Coaching is not an option, it's a requirement of Servant Leaders. The question is how to coach effectively to influence and achieve the desired results.

To actively coach there are five steps:
1. Tell them.
2. Show them.
3. Do it with them.
4. Have them do it.
5. Show appreciation and give encouragement.

Note: loop back as often as necessary.

There are three objectives in professional coaching:

1. Educate
2. Train
3. Inspire

Yes, it's possible to accomplish all three objectives when coaching, although it's helpful to focus on one of the three as the lead purpose. The following are a few examples of coaching:

- I was walking down the hallway with a divisional VP when we approached a younger associate walking and texting. Coaching opportunity in the moment: the senior executive said with a friendly smile, "Excuse me, could I ask you to stop and step to the side to finish your important communication, thank you."

- An escort and I were walking across the floor of a nuclear power plant facility when we needed to take five steps up and down to cross a large pipe. At the top, my escort coached me, "John, on our way down could I ask you to hold on to the handrail. The reason why…."

- On the second day of a training event, after a team member gave the safety debrief, the leader asked the group what else should be added to the agenda after making observations during the first day of the event. Three additional issues were added.

- The chief financial officer (CFO) of a company scheduled a coaching session with three newly hired accountants so she could walk through and show them how to post depreciation of equipment.

- As the leader walked by, he heard an associate answering the phone abruptly, sounding more like he was being interrupted rather than welcoming the call with enthusiasm. The leader reminded the associate how each call should be handled as if he had the opportunity to talk to and listen to the most important person in the world.

- The manager of a service department stopped and took two minutes to show a technician the proper way to hold a tool to get the most torque to tighten or loosen a bolt.
- A grocery store manager on his morning walk around stopped and took some extra time in the meat department, asking questions and showing a better way to display T-Bone steaks.
- A CEO walked into an engineering scheduling meeting; prior to stepping out, he raised his hand and asks, "I wonder what would happen if we…"
- A surgeon working in a teaching hospital in the middle of a challenging operation told a student to let go of the clamps, hold the artery, and don't move.

My point: coaching can be formal or informal, can be directive or supportive, can be done in two minutes or two hours—we as Servant Leaders need to do it often and well.

When in doubt—*Should I coach or not?*—the answer is almost always, *Yes, and right now in the moment.* Coaching must be intentional and purposeful and it must be the mindset of the leader to look for obvious coaching opportunities, and believe me, they are everywhere. With that understanding, the timing of coaching is important. For example, our coaching should never purposefully embarrass another person; so coaching in public where they might be embarrassed should be avoided, when possible. Also, during a crisis, coaching should be postponed—unless life or death situations are at stake. Sometimes it's appropriate to ask permission, "Is this a good time?" If not, then, "When would be a better time?" Or, "How about early tomorrow?"

When coaching, always explain "what" is being coached and "why" it's important to them and others. When appropriate, always use examples, demonstrations, or illustrations to drive home the importance of improvement.

Why Not?

The question is why do we *not* coach?

One reason we don't coach is because of the negative experiences when others didn't want to be coached. Or our style of coaching was too predictable and we were tuned out. Answer: hit the refresh button and look for different ways to communicate by building positive segues or doing a better job of framing why and what needs to improve. Ask people how they like to be coached to improve performance and results. Also, after coaching, ask for feedback. "Was the coaching the other day helpful?" If not, ask, "What could have been said or done to achieve better results?"

The second reason I hear most often is time. We get so caught up in our day-to-day tasks that we fail to make coaching a priority—then it's viewed as an interruption versus value added and a most important aspect of being a leader. My point of view is that we should always be coaching and always looking for opportunities to coach.

We should be *supportive* in our coaching style versus *directive*; however, at times directive coaching is required. I have been told that if we are 80 percent supportive, those we coach will allow us to be directive 20 percent of the time. The key to solving the time management issue is to prioritize coaching, and yes, actually put it on the must-do list.

There are a few dos and don'ts to remember when coaching:

Do	Don't
• Coach in the moment when possible. • Ask permission when coaching up. • Always ask for feedback after they tried it your way. • Give verbal and nonverbal positive reinforcement. • Make coaching point easy to correct. • Plan it when possible. • Be aware of circumstances of the person, team, and situation before coaching. • Talk about your own challenges of the coaching issue.	• Lose your temper • Argue • Embarrass someone in front of others • Give off nonverbal signs of impatience • Belittle others while coaching • Make fun of the person's lack of understanding

Stage 3 – Partnering

There are times when doing an activity, task, or improving a skill is beneficial when done together, and perhaps over an extended period. Partnering is a stage that flows up to coaching and down to delegating. Partnering may become an important function of both coaching and delegating. Let's put the spotlight on partnering and unpack it to see the power in it for the Level V Servant Leader.

Many times, individuals need to see it or watch you handle all the non-descriptive activities of an activity. I had a physician tell me once that he could teach me in a classroom in ten minutes how to remove an appendix—but it would take him years to help me learn all that is needed to be done when something goes wrong. In fact, no one has ever written a guide about how to respond when something goes wrong; so they need to watch and work with other physicians to see how to respond when it does. This is partnering.

Another reminder. My friend Dr. David Durkin, an anesthesiologist, has told me often, "John, I'm not paid to put people to sleep, I'm paid the big bucks to wake them up." Again, same point; only through watching and partnering will I see enough cases that will help me be successful.

In our business, presenting workshops and training sessions are great opportunities for partnering. I can give anyone an outline, but the difference in actually conducting a workshop and facilitating one with impact is always the transition from one topic to the next. So, we partner, or tandem, to demonstrate the transitions, the connecting points, and the things that tie concepts together.

Key Concept

Partnering must be attached to either coaching or delegating—it should not stand alone. In other words, I've watched partnering where the leader demonstrated the skill and then assumed that because the associate has seen it, now they get it. Not true. Recently, I made this mistake. I had an associate ask me to show him how to "cold call" companies and organizations to help sell public classes. We spent an afternoon walking into businesses, and after about four hours, he had at least eight opportunities for follow-up. Because we were so excited about the results, I made the mistake of thinking that my associate now understood the art of cold calling. I didn't link it to coaching: watching him do it and assigning expectations. Thus, after the follow-up with the eight potential prospects, everything came to a halt.

Two Skills

Allow me a brief pause between Stages 3 and 4 to mention two skills needed throughout the six-stage process to becoming a Servant Leader—feedback and apology. Both skills are highlighted in what I believe to be one of the greatest coaching books ever written: *What Got You Here Won't Get You There* by Marshall Goldsmith, the title alone is valuable. Goldsmith gives great insight into getting and giving feedback and making an apology.[1]

Feedback – Feedback is the concept of feeding forward. Not the old rehash of a painful past—rather, let's get busy moving people toward their exciting futures. So, the framing of feedback might sound like this, "Joe, as we look to your future in the next four months, here are two areas you will want to improve to make you an even more effective leader. Consider...." Or when asking for feedback, "Mike, I have always appreciated your coaching. I was wondering about _____. What could I work on in the next sixty days that would help me be more effective?"

The Apology – I love Goldsmith's perspective: keep it simple and keep it real. Do not dig your hole any bigger when you need to apologize; just say, "I'm sorry." Then add, "I'll try to do better in the future."[2]

Stage 4 – Delegating

The heart and soul of professional development is delegating. It's not work distribution; instead, it must be an opportunity where you select, assign, and sell to the individual for connecting to his or her development or succession plan. When you delegate, you do not advocate responsibility at this stage; but it is your goal when you deputize (explained later in Stage 5).

When delegation is used for work distribution, it's viewed as "dumping" on steroids. Everyone in the workforce has been "dumped on," at one time or another. It leaves us feeling like our names were picked out of a hat or we were perceived by the boss as having the least responsibilities and dumping on us was an easy way out for the boss. Maybe it was something the boss didn't want to do or didn't want to make the time to do. Anyone in our department could have completed the task, but for no good reason, we were elected.

The Servant Leader will identify two ways to effectively delegate. Note: both ways are for the benefit of others and not necessarily smooth sailing for you, because you can count on mistakes to be made.

The first way is to identify an area or issue that needs to be addressed that will help your team or department improve its productivity and efficiencies. Then look for someone on your team who taking on this challenge fits with their performance plan and development plan.

The second way is to identify the person by reviewing their development plan and overall performance; what issue or area would benefit the team to advance and be a win in developing their skills and abilities.

Both cases present huge opportunities for coaching and development for the individual. In a perfect world, every direct report would have a delegation opportunity that you are working with them on to advance their skill in their performance plans.

With these scenarios in mind, delegation then requires all our selling, human relations, and planning skills. It cannot be "winged," it must be intentional to produce the desired outcomes—a project that advances the team and an individual win in spearheading the results.

After the key issue or task has been identified and the associate has agreed and officially delegated, the next two steps are critical for the success of the project and the accountability to achieve the desired outcome. To effectively sell the development of the associate and advancement of the organizational goal is tied to the core issue or task, the delegator designs a draft plan or framework of the planning process. Now it's important to take the framework and work with the delegate to finalize the plan. In other words, complete in detail and make it theirs.

The critical factor is together to see in detail the desired outcome and all its functions and impact on the stakeholders. Do we see the same picture? Do not move ahead until this is clearly understood from both perspectives. Then you can move on to defining the current reality. This creates planning tension between the desired outcomes and the current reality. Only when this tension exists can you then move together to determine goals and milestones and clear actions to move from reality to a new desired state.

Now that you have goals and actions or strategies, we need to establish resource allocation to truly unleash the talents of your associates. Time, talent, and treasure are required for success. Now we have time stamps associated with each action with agreed upon deliverables. This is where Level IV and V leaders establish accountability up stream so that when a problem arises we have time to adjust and implement contingency plans.

Therefore, the final step is to agree upon appropriate feedback sequences: how, when, who, and most importantly, what will be reviewed. If this is agreed upon at the front end, then it's baked into the process to be helpful rather than after the fact when it feels like big brother is watching over and controlling the project.

Also, the feedback process is a natural way for the leader to coach, partner, or even move ahead to raise the bar. During regularly scheduled feedback meetings, coaching should always be done so that you can prepare to deputize the process to the delegated associate.

Key point in delegation: as the leader, you are still responsible and accountable for all outcomes—good and bad. It becomes a tremendous development opportunity for your associates, because you will not allow them to fail. This creates a win-win opportunity for you as the Servant Leader. They will become empowered and you all will reap the harvest. Remember, it's not about you it's always about others.

Stage 5 – Deputizing

A few years ago, working as a Level II leader, I was frustrated with an associate who was not working anywhere near his potential. My solution was to continue to tell him what he needed to do and hold him accountable by turning in sales activity reports. This tactic, of course, was a disaster because he seldom turned in reports, and when he did, they were incomplete. This led to a shouting match and a human relation violation. If there was a human relations referee present, there would have been multiple flags, and I might have been thrown out of the game. Of course, being a good Level II boss, I felt justified in shouting because he deserved it and it was for his good.

As I later reflected on that day—as I was being challenged to think differently in seeing, planning, communicating, coaching, correcting, and becoming a Level V leader—I thought, *I was only thinking about me, not my associate.* Breakthrough moment!

What I discovered as I began to move to more Level V thinking is that in developing others it was not about how I liked to be coached, tell, and partner—instead, it was more important to determine how *others* wanted and needed to be coached. It was about a month later when I realized that my associate, when it came to business development, wanted to be deputized.

Therefore, I eliminated all the activity reports and daily and weekly sales quotas. Then I had him raise his right hand and swear to do the best he could do and he would call when he needed help. In six months, he went from the middle of the pack to top ten in North America sales, and top twenty globally.

The analogy comes from the old Western films. The bank robbers ride into town, rob the bank, and leave town with all the money and guns blazing. The town sheriff gathers all the men of the town in front of his office, passes out deputy badges, then has them raise their right hand and swear to uphold the law as part of the posse to find the bank robbers and more importantly get their money back. Then they would race for their horses and off they went, empowered by the badge. Note: they were deputized for a specific task or opportunity, after the mission was accomplished, they turned in their badges.

In business, we do not necessarily turn in our badges if the task or activity continues to benefit the team or organization. Many times, people are recruited to be deputized to own a task, which will be outlined in their job description. In the development process, deputizing is the goal of delegation because responsibility can be passed on; in the delegation process, the leader is still responsible. Also, after a person is knighted or deputized, the leader can still raise the bar and, when necessary, partner, coach, or communicate. Another way to understand deputizing is that the ownership of the project, task, or activity has been passed on from the leader to the associate.

Stage 6 – Raising the Bar

Right now, wherever you are, I want you to drop what you are reading and raise your hand as high as you can. Good job—perhaps you needed the stretch. Now do it again but raise your hand another three inches. It's always interesting to me that when I make this request in a group setting, everyone takes on the challenge, and then can actually reach another three inches higher. We can always reach higher—believe it.

It takes a leader to establish the rapport and trust to have all the team members rise to the next level—or to "raise the bar." This phrase comes from a track and field event where athletes keep jumping or vaulting higher and higher over a bar until only one person has cleared the highest height. In life and work, we talk ourselves into what is high enough or how hard we want to work. These limitations are almost always in the eye of the beholder—unless a Servant Leader can expose the potential and the person chooses to rise to the challenge of becoming more.

Aspects of life that can influence our beliefs as to what is possible:

- Up-bringing
- Past experiences
- Previous jobs
- Previous managers
- Generational differences
- Tiredness
- Health

The Servant Leader creates in subordinates an eager want or desire to improve and get better. Level I-III leaders just tell people to improve and make clear the negative consequences if they don't achieve the desired results. Level III leaders might think about rewards if successful and consequences of failure, but they seldom carry out threats.

Returning to our engagement thinking in Chapter 1, associates feel more engaged when they feel valued, appreciated, and inspired to accomplish more, faster, better, with fewer resources. So, raising the bar is tied to *how*.

As Level V Servant Leaders, unlocking the abilities of people around us by raising the bar is nothing short of a conversation, asking questions and throwing down challenges. Due to the trust, respect, and credibility we have established, others will be motivated to exceed expectations of their leader.

Accountability

Accountability is at the heart of the Servant Leader. Creating in others an "eager want" is a core Dale Carnegie human relation principle taught in his book, *How to Win Friends and Influence People*. This core principle is the cornerstone of accountability for the Servant Leader.

Let's examine the accountability thought process based on the five levels of leadership:

5 Levels of Leadership - Holding Others Accountable

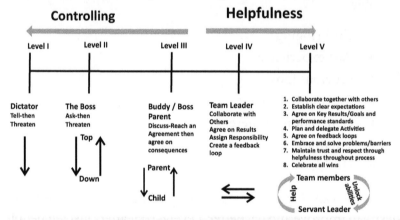

Level I Accountability. At Level I, accountability has a range from a direct threat of some negative action—perhaps even as high as losing a job—to making others feel that a dire consequence will take place, even if not stated directly. This, of course, starts with the directive without questioning what is to be accomplished. Interesting to me, those who have a desire to please people respond to this style of accountability. In fact, wanting to please the boss is their motivation. Years later, they enjoy telling their war stories with others, even tending to glorify the experience. What can never be measured is the "what if" or the "what could have been" if accountability was shared.

Level II Accountability is the same as Level I accountability; the difference here is the boss will ask some questions and may discuss, but the threat is just as intense.

Level III Accountability. Level III accountability is when the Level III leader, the buddy or parent, engages in dialog and reaches an agreement about what needs to be accomplished and the consequences if the agreement is not accomplished. Here the Level III range is influenced by the degree the agreement is more or less collaborative in nature. Both parties have a great feeling of satisfaction and even excitement over their mutually agreed results, and even the consequences even if they are dire in nature. The challenge is that when the results are not met, then the buddy or parents must punish their buddy or child and the child becomes disenchanted and no longer can fully trust the Level III leader. Bottom line at this level: there is very little or zero accountability. The simple result is that in this relationship we tend to just move the standard to what is in line with what is happening, rather than reaching for what we need to make happen.

Note the shift in thinking as we move from Level III to Level IV and V. In the final two levels, standards are discussed and then agreed upon and will not change unless overwhelming evidence is presented to adjust the standards. However, standards will never be adjusted based on nonperformance. Also, the focus is off the individual, and we think more as a team. The shift from "me" to "we" is evident.

Level IV Accountability. The team leader at Level IV seeks others' thoughts and facts that help them work toward a collaborative, reasonable result or agreement. Here a collaborative, attainable result is agreed upon. Then responsibilities of all stakeholders are assigned with timetables and an acceptable feedback loop agreed to by all involved. This way, changes and adjustments can be made during the process.

Accountability, or allegiance, is to the team, not to a personal reward or recognition. Evidence seems to support we go the extra mile when team members' success is at stake, not just our own wins because we tend to justify our current situation. However, in being other-focused, helping the team win is far more motivating for putting forth extra discretionary efforts.

Level V Accountability. The Servant Leader follows *eight steps of accountability:*

1. Collaborate with others. In this step, we collaboratively seek facts and others' thoughts to achieve the goal. The Servant Leader understands that "People support a world that they help create." So with this thought in mind, the Level V leader will facilitate a discussion through whatever means is available, possible, and acceptable to all involved. Obviously, face to face is best, next is a conference call, next is an email chain, or even through social media; for example, a twitter discussion may prove effective. Regardless, getting as many people participating in the discussion so we get all the information the good, bad, and ugly to make an intelligent, informed decision on appropriate actions. The key here is that fear is gone between individuals and different roles in the organization because the focus is on the data.

2. Establish clear expectations. Establishing clear expectations of the team becomes the heart of the Servant Leader. Here the picture must be clear of what the finished activity, report, task, job, or outcome looks like. Servant Leaders understand that to be helpful they must share with others exactly the same picture and understanding of what good looks like.

I was coaching a senior executive team that was meeting outside Philadelphia in a high-end hotel, discussing specific strategy to complete a business turnaround. There were nine executives in the room when an action was stated, one that involved the operations VP who had a specific action and a series of tasks to complete. After discussion, it was agreed that the operations VP would conduct operational training critical to achieving the plant's quarterly goals.

It was amazingly obvious to me that everyone who had to take zero action became more and more excited about the potential results. I smiled to myself because I knew the operations VP was not buying into it for a minute. He had other stresses that were far more reaching than training in this particular area. Then the

CEO asked who was in agreement and every head nodded yes, even the operations VP. "Great," said the CEO, "this will be accomplished in the next six weeks; let's move on."

I raised my hand and said, "Sorry to stop the presses, but we have an issue. All nine of you agreed, and eight of you actually believe that in the next six weeks this training will be completed, right?"

Again every head nodded yes.

Then I asked the operations VP, "Do you have any intention whatsoever of accomplishing this task?"

"NO," he said bluntly.

The next 30 minutes of the session were spent on how the other Vice Presidents could become more helpful to the Operations Vice President so that the important task could be achieved.

You see, it's not just understanding the expectation, there must be total buy-in agreement to meeting the expectation.

3. Agree on key results/goals and performance standards. Every expectation must have clear goals and standards. In my work as a Dale Carnegie trainer, we refer to business goals as key results, and each key result has to have a measurable performance standard. In other words, what prompts a celebration?

4. Plan and delegate activities. For each goal and performance standard, we need a plan of action with an understanding of who, how, and when. The Level V Servant Leader understands it starts with *who*. These are the individuals who will accomplish the plan, not just the established agreed upon expectation and goal. Now we are back to people skills: who do we assign, etc. No! Rather, who do we sell for the purpose of growth, or perhaps it's just work distribution and it's the alignment of skills and talents. Regardless, people must be sold by talking in terms of their benefits that we already know because we have been building a trusting relationship prior to this step.

5. Agree on feedback loops. Now that we have the who, how, and when established, next the Servant Leader needs to reach agreement on appropriate feedback times and methods. If we fail here, we run the chance that the team will feel controlled and overmanaged, which will result in lower engagement levels. This is an important step because the Servant Leader will need this information to better serve or to be helpful to the peer group and perhaps the leader or boss.

6. Embrace and solve problems/barriers. Feedback will alert the Level V Servant Leaders when there are problems that might impact future deadlines. The Servant Leader does not dread problems, but embraces them and is even more excited to be made aware of them in order to be helpful. Remember, being helpful the majority of the time is to do nothing but perhaps ask a few questions, allowing the people you have delegated this responsibility to to solve their own problems. Do not buy them back. Discerning when to engage and when not to engage in problem solving is an important competency of a Servant Leader.

Helping others see and take personal ownership is more important for the Servant Leader than in actually solving the problem. However, when solving or coaching your people to solve problems, keep it simple. I like what Dale Carnegie taught about solving problems by asking four simple questions:[3]

1. What is the problem?
2. What is the cause of the problem? (green light)
3. What are all possible solutions to the problem? (with evidence)
4. What is the best solution to the problem? (with strong evidence)

7. Maintain trust and respect through helpfulness throughout process. The Servant Leader cannot be helpful if he or she loses trust and respect with the leader or the team. A year ago, it was my privilege to be on a radio show with Joel Peterson, the former President of Jet Blue. We were discussing his book *The 10 Laws of Trust*. His perspective of building trust is right on. Here are three of his thoughts:

- Knowledge of the subject matter at hand. Note: I trust my mother, but not to fly a plane.
- Authority to provide the resources to be successful (time, talent, treasure)
- Character strength (I got your back)

8. Celebrate all wins. It's important to celebrate all wins, including the milestones along the way. Everyone appreciates acknowledging the hard work it takes to reach a goal. The changes we must make in the process is really the difference between actually achieving the result—or not. So, celebrate the positive shifts in thinking and the progress made, paving the pathways for personal and team success.

As the Servant Leader follows these eight steps to achieve accountability, it allows the leader to be helpful versus controlling. It allows the Servant Leader to have various opportunities to influence further up-stream before something or someone becomes a critical factor in the success of the task, job, requirement, or project.

If you follow this line of thinking, the Servant Leader is accountable to the team to follow the process and never abdicates 100 percent responsibility for the desired outcome. As the Servant Leader follows the eight steps, he or she is truly being helpful to all team members; in return, the team unleashes their talents, abilities, discretionary energy, and time toward the outcome. In fact, putting forth every effort is never an issue. Result: fully engaged associates. Ahhh…sweet!

Alan Mulally, in a talk he gave at the Dale Carnegie 69th International convention in 2016, made a point that when you are asking another person to change or to collaborate, be sure it's an invitation not a demand. Servant Leaders invite people to join them to change behavior. Then it's their choice; if they choose not to engage, it's okay. Perhaps they would fit better in another organization and be much happier.

Onward !

Summary

First described in the book *Think and Grow Rich* by Napoleon Hill, when Charles Darby introduced himself to Thomas Edison, Darby said years later about their first meeting, "He had the look and smell of a tramp, but the mind of a king...." We will define breakthrough as a significant advance, not a stretch. Look to challenging yourself with "the mind of a king," so you then can influence others to pursue breakthrough results in life and work.

Key Questions

1. *What is your current 3x breakthrough plan for your life and work?*

2. *How do you inspire breakthrough results in others?*

3. *How does accountability change when wearing Servant Leader lenses?*

4. *When wearing Servant Leader lenses, how does your role in developing people change?*

5. *What will be your new plan to delegate and or assign work looking through the lenses of a Servant Leader?*

Endnotes

1. Marshal Goldsmith, *What Got You Here Won't Get You There: How Successful People Become Even More Successful* (New York: Hyperion, 2007), 111-141.
2. Ibid, 141.
3. Dale Carnegie, *How to Stop Worrying and Start Living* (New York, Simon and Shuster, 1948).

CHAPTER 8

Becoming Other-Focused

Opportunity is where you find it, not where it finds you.
– Peter Drucker

In 2012, our family had the opportunity to participate in a family mission trip together, and we went to Haiti. Our family joined a group who had established a mission in Haiti—Poverty Resolution, operated by Matt and Andrew Jones. Based on our abilities, we had various projects to work on during the week. It was a tremendous experience, serving together and creating another family memory.

One activity I was asked to do on three afternoons was to lead a leadership retreat for local village leaders and pastors serving the area. I was more than surprised when I walked into the room to see thirty-plus people sitting there with pens and tablets ready, wanting to learn from "the American." I soon discovered that the village leaders and pastors were many times the very same person, with perhaps little skill or knowledge about either function. I did my best through an interpreter.

I started with asking a few questions such as why they came, what did they hope to learn, and why that was important to them. That way I could to tailor my remarks to be beneficial. I talked briefly about the differences in leading; focusing either on others or self. This struck a nerve with them and led to the how-to discussion where I introduced them to ten or so Dale Carnegie human relation principles.

The reason I share this story is what happened after the last session on the third day. I noticed an older man who was interested and at time I wasn't sure if I was reading into the situation, but he seemed to have tears in his eyes. He approached me and, through an interpreter, wanted to thank me—that I had been a five-year answer to prayer. He said that although he walked four hours one-way for the last three days, it was worth every step. As the village leader and pastor, he knew the laws of the village and he knew Scripture, but he never understood that his role was truly about helping others. Furthermore, he now was realizing that it was not what others needed from him but rather for them to know that someone cared and loved them.

This conversation was humbling for me. To be honest I thought meeting with these leaders would be meaningless. How could they possibly relate to me and I to them? See it? I was focused on me, not them. Then I receive this heartfelt feedback and I realize the impact I had—anyone can have, if we focus on others. As I flew home from that trip, I wondered who might have I missed because my focus was on "me" not "we." John Maxwell wrote a book titled, *Failing Forward*. What a great concept, especially for those of us on the journey to becoming a Servant Leader.

This them-not-me concept is easy to understand but challenging to apply. It sounds so wonderful, but goes counter to our nature. Therefore, becoming a Servant Leader is a process—not an event or a single decision. Failure will happen often, but must not derail your efforts. Always keep in mind the rewards of being a Servant Leader not just to yourself but to all people in your life.

Fear Be Gone

Isn't it interesting that almost everything that causes frustration, fear, worry, and stress is due to being self-focused rather than being other focused? Recently I was coaching an executive who was wrought with fear about a speech he was giving to board members and other stakeholders. I asked the person, "In thinking about your fear, who are you thinking about?"

After a few seconds of thought, the person replied, "I'm thinking of myself."

"Ok," I said, "let's turn the tables. Let's think about your audience and what they need to hear to make better decisions."

Later I received a nice thank you note.

All in the Family

The competitiveness of siblings in family businesses never ceases to amaze me. But I enjoy working with family businesses because nothing is more exciting than to see the torch successfully passed from one generation to the next. Regardless, in the spirited rivalry, it's most difficult to be about others' success. On the contrary, due to sibling positioning, it can tear families and businesses apart. Same antidote: when you are at the height of frustration within a family business, stop and analyze who are you focused on. Remember, it's not about you, it's about others. If you are in a challenging family business going through a difficult time, you probably just threw this book at the wall and walked away. It's that hard.

Many years ago, I found myself in the middle of a family crisis. My grandparents both had passed on, and their estate was in the process of being passed down. After six years of challenges, it was becoming clear as to what the options were in being able to move forward. It happens that our family was given the first opportunity to sell our current home and buy my grandparents eight-acre estate with all the trimmings. I was so excited to move back home, I would have a house double the size for our growing family of five children. I would have eight acres to live on with a pool and tennis courts! I thought I had hit the lotto. In my story, have you noticed how often the word "I" has appeared?

In reality, it made a lot more sense for my sister Joy and her husband Keith to live in my grandparents' home. And my wife Colleen had some major concerns about us moving. The hardest decision I made in my life was to deny my wants and desires and do what was right for others: Colleen and my children and my sister Joy and her family. All my frustration and anger was totally focused on me. However, when I made the shift to what was best for others, I can't even describe to you the peace of mind, happiness, and relief that came with shifting my focus to "we" and away from "me."

Selfishness Blinds Us in Being about Others

We want what we want when we want it. This is why becoming a Servant Leader and learning to be about others is so hard. Allow me to expand your thinking in becoming other-focused. Please note being other-focused is not just something we turn on and off when we go to work so that we will get better results. If it's not in your DNA, others will in time smoke it out and you will lose credibility, then respect and then trust. With that in mind, the following are decisions that we make every day that either reflect a self-focus or other-focus:

- If you attend church, is it about you or others?
- Where you attend church and why? Is it within your comfort zone or helpful and meaningful to others?
- What kind of music do you listen to at home, in the car? What is your favorite?
- Where do you stop to eat when traveling or just going out for dinner?
- Is it appropriate to order alcohol? What if you know someone at your table is struggling with addiction?
- Do you discipline your children?
- Do you complain when asked to help with household chores?
- Do you answer the phone while sitting at dinner with your family? Who is important?
- Are you preoccupied with a football game rather than enjoying Thanksgiving dinner?
- Who chooses where and what you are going to do on vacation? Do you think of others' desires?

- Do you proactively work at developing meaning friendships? It takes effort and denial of self-interest.
- When with friends, do you listen more than talk? Can you learn to just *be* with others?
- Do you tease people in public, sometimes at their expense? Do you think it is fun to be the life of the party?
- When planning your monthly budget, are you only focused on your needs, wants, desires?
- When saving for retirement, whose needs are you considering? Yours or others even beyond family?

Key point. In becoming a Servant Leader you are learning to deny self and become more focused on others. In our personal lives is where we can practice the most, and it will take the most time. I still cringe at some of the things I used to focus on in my life.

Onward!

Note: My faith walk has been the most help to me in embracing this truth of servant leadership. My point of view is from the Christian tradition. As I continue to deepen my faith, which is a journey not an event, I have learned about helpfulness through a spiritual lens. As a Christian, I strive to follow the teachings of Jesus; although I fail often, my intent of followership never waivers. Jesus talks about loving others, which is the spiritual side of the helpfulness coin. The apostle Paul in his letter written to the Galatians states that all the laws previously written can be summed up in the following two: Love God and love others. Saint Augustine, an early Church historian in AD 300, simply says there are three rules for living: "Love God, love others, and then live your life however you want." My personal motto.

Andy Stanley, senior pastor of a megachurch in Atlanta, Georgia, delivered a message series called "Brand New" in which he challenges all of us when faced with difficult circumstances to always ask the most powerful filtering question: "What does love require?" In the past year, I have applied this simple principle to all my challenges, and it's amazing—within a few minutes or less the answer and subsequent actions become quite clear, and most times quite painful.

Perhaps for you, becoming other-focused might not be a faith conviction that will help you make the mind shift from "me" to "we," the ability to deny self. A friend of mine who is not religious tells me that if we just apply the Dale Carnegie human relation principle of appealing to the nobler motives in what is right, honorable, and true, that being other-focused just makes so much sense.

Summary

Servant Leaders make a major mind shift from "me" to "we," which continually needs to be reinforced for the rest of their lives. When you wake in the morning, are your first thoughts of yourself or others? When getting ready to leave in the morning, are your thoughts self-absorbed or are you thinking the best for others? Do you hope the coffee is on for your gratification or are you hoping you will be able to start the coffee machine to better serve others? I understand it's impossible to always have the other mindset; okay, so let's go back to percentages. What would happen if we thought of others more, and less of ourselves?

Key Questions

1. *What major decision are you facing that by denying self and focusing on others will make the decision-making process very clear?*

2. *What self-centered mindsets do you need to remove from your life that might block your progress in becoming a Servant Leader?*

3.   What role does your faith have in your ability to understand the servant mindset?

4.   How hard is it for you to tell others you love them? If it is hard, why is it hard?

5.   When evaluating your day, do you think first of your accomplishments or about how you helped others succeed?

CHAPTER 9

Committed to Developing
Others First

*What I keep saying is, don't be the person who has all
the answers; be the person who has the best questions.
And then you'll get better answers!*
– James A. Autry, Practicing Servant Leadership

Take out a sheet of paper. Draw a line down the middle. On the left side of the paper, list all the people in whom you trust the most. After you have written eight to ten names, stop and think about each person, *Why do I trust this person?* Then move to the right side of the paper and list all the people who have been and who are helpful to you. What are you learning? If you have similar results as those in my classes and coaching assignments, you are discovering that the same people are on both lists. It's easier to coach people to be helpful than to be trustworthy. On the other hand, if I can coach you to become truly helpful, I then can coach you to build trust.

I was recently in a meeting in Boston where a team of international business people were discussing branding, where leadership was a core value. Because of their discussion, they believed that the term "helpfulness" was weak, it lacked executive leadership power. I was just listening, it was not my place or role to influence others; at the time I was just an observer. Beyond a potential language barrier, I would have welcomed the opportunity to challenge their thinking.

Let's take a deep dive into helpful.

Helpful Defined

Being helpful means making it easier to do a job or deal with a problem. Giving or rendering aid or assistance; of service:

- Helpfulness is the DNA of a Servant Leader the opposite of controlling.
- Synonyms: useful, convenient; beneficial, advantageous
- Per Thesaurus.com, the word helpful has an additional 44 synonyms

Questions: Of the adjectives used to define helpful, how many of those words describe you? If you were on trial today, would you be found guilty by a jury of your peers for living out the "helpful" characteristics? Take each word and ask yourself, *What would being helpful look like in my personal and professional life? What behaviors should I consider changing to be considered helpful?*

I was invited to a wedding in Haiti taking place over the Thanksgiving holiday. I wasn't interested in going, in fact I decided not to go. My wife, Colleen, and daughters Jackie, Jillian, and Kaitrin are going. Our son Sam and our daughter Alex and their families are not going, so I'm not going. I personally struggle with the Haitian culture and mindsets. Although my heart breaks every time I visit an orphanage, it just is not my ideal place to visit during Thanksgiving week. Hmmm…so who am I focused on? What about my niece who is getting married and her parents? What about my family members who are going, what message am I sending them?

I needed a paradigm shift to realize that it's not about me and my desires, likes, and dislikes. My decision should be about others and being helpful (fill in any of the adjectives) to others. It did not take long for me to realize, once I shifted away from self, that I should go to the wedding in Haiti.

Temperament

The Servant Leader temperament is interesting to review. The concept of temperament was popularized during the United States presidential election between Hillary Clinton and Donald Trump. The context was that each candidate challenged the other about having the right temperament to be president. What they were asking voters to consider was, does she or he have the right emotional maturity to act presidential?

Temperament is a person's nature, especially as it permanently affects their behavior; therefore, it's an innate characteristic—how you naturally respond to different situations and people under normal conditions and under stressful conditions as well. If you are aware of your temperament, you can adjust your inherent inclinations. Psychologists believe that a dramatic event, a life-and-death situation, a horrific abusive situation, or even a dramatic religious conversion can alter temperament and how we respond to different situations.

There are hundreds of tests you can take ranging from elementary to highly detailed to determine your dominate temperament. Most tests divide people into four quadrants and help determine which temperament types are dominate or recessive. Note: The results are not good or bad, just helpful so the Servant Leader can study temperament to better serve others by either adjusting their own temperament to better lead others or to read others' temperaments to better connect, coach, delegate, encourage, or appreciate in more meaningful ways.

Key Point: It's a mindset of servicing others, not a personal temperament that makes us Servant Leaders.

Personally, I am biased toward the DISC instruments of testing. In my close work with the team at Bartell & Bartell, I learned to best read and understand the DISC under normal conditions and then under stress. Also in my work with the Bartell team, I began to look for patterns, almost like a temperament DNA, to acquire better insights into others. The following are just a few high-level insights:

- D-Driver: the high Driver person is all about urgency and getting things done quickly showing little if any people sensitivity.
- I-Influencer: the high Influencer person is the conversationalist or talker, will chat with anyone at any time.
- S-Stabilizer: the high Stabilizer person is sensitive to people, what they are thinking or feeling.
- C-Conscientious: the high Conscientious person is all about detail.

Other personality traits that you can change with time and can be specifically measured regarding developing a coaching plan are areas like the following:

- Do you see many solutions to a problem or just one? Flexible or fixed?
- Are you organized or disorganized?
- Are you reserved or outgoing?
- Is your motivation internal or external?
- Is your perceived self-worth high or low?
- How assertive are you—bold or obliging?
- Is your interpersonal style extrovert or introvert?
- Are you cooperative? Competitive or accommodating?
- Are you a risk-seeker to averse to taking risks?
- How is your mental toughness—tough-minded or self-sensitive?

All of these points are samplings of Bartell & Bartell executive instruments. Temperament and individual personality traits are important to Servant Leaders to help them focus on blind spots in their own lives and begin to take correction. Just as important as adjusting your actions, you can also have your team profiled, which provides accurate analysis of their personality traits—with amazingly scary precision. This information helps us to truly be about others when we can customize how we tell, coach, partner, deputize, and raise the bar.

It will give us insights as to how people like to get feedback and take corrective action in holding them accountable for results. Remember, people do not think and respond like you do. In fact, everyone is different in certain ways. Understanding how others are wired will give you the competitive edge in your pursuit to becoming a Servant Leader.

Recently I was coaching an executive. She was constantly challenged when working with one of her managers. She has a high D temperament, always wanting to get to the point, solve the problem, and move on. She is learning to sit on her D temperament and take time to reconnect with her associates. One morning her challenged manager walked into her office, interrupting her current train of thought and started to ramble about his girlfriend problems after two failed marriages at age 55. She told me that at first she was furious—how dare he come in and waste my time with his nonsense. Then it hit her, *Who am I focused on? Me.* So she put down her pen and the spreadsheets she was reviewing, got up from her desk, and said, "Come on, let's go get some coffee." The result? She built trust and respect with the manager. Trust and respect are two needed helpers when it comes to coaching and raising the performance bar. Over the next two weeks, this manager brought her three different ideas how to increase revenues in his department. Other-focused, not self.

Being Helpful

Reminder: it's not if you think you have been helpful or it's not what you think based on your knowledge is helpful, rather from their point of view what would be helpful to them. Here is an example of a perceived helpful email I sent to my administrative bookkeeper.

> *AGAIN, THE NUMBERS SEEM TO OFF IN OUR*
> *MONTHLY FRANCHISE REPORT. PLEASE ADJUST.*
> *Thank you,*
> *JR*

I thought this email was helpful, and I even thanked her for the revised spreadsheet. You can imagine my surprise when I learned she left the office in tears exclaiming, "I can never do anything right." Sometimes we should just know better like this email, which was in all capital letters, which meant to the bookkeeper that I was yelling at her. Other times we need to get in the habit of asking for help in getting feedback: Was this meeting, correspondence, statement, coaching helpful? If not, what could I have done or said that would have been more helpful to you or the team?

Not every time will helpfulness feel helpful in the moment to an individual or to your team. Here we must use discernment as to how much time is needed to get the feedback and from whom. For example, when you think it is necessary to ask for a performance review, it may not feel helpful to the associate in question at the time, but it's still the right thing to do for that person's future success. When the person is back on track, he or she will eventually come around and thank you. If you need to remove people from the project or company, it might take longer for them to see they were not in the right seat and now they are functioning differently and better in another team or organization. The heart of the matter is that the Servant Leader needs to serve by being other-focused and not making decisions from self-centeredness.

Another interesting discovery for me is how inflexible untrained leaders are, it's actually humorous. We get caught in patterns. If something was successful or perceived as successful, we will continue to do it again and again. The adage applies: your past successes pave the way to your future failures. Success may cause a false sense of believing your actions and words are helpful today because they were helpful last week or yesterday. Maybe yesterday's coaching was the right stage to be working with your associates, but today they need to be partnered with someone else. Maybe last year your team met a short-term goal because you got their attention with a stern lecture on hard work. So, you believe that stern lectures which turn into shouting is the key to success. If we assume what worked last week or last year will work today, we are self-focused, not other-focused and not helpful.

Have you ever wondered why an emergency vehicle's siren varies in tone? The human ear will tune out a monotone. To get and keep attention on the alarm, we hear a shrill whistle that goes up and down the scale. Believe me, I know. I lived next to a fire station while attending college. The point in leadership is variety. If we get past what is convenient for us and focus more on what is beneficial for others, we will bring tremendous variety into our understanding of being a Servant Leader.

Trust, Respect, Credibility

A Servant Leader's daily mindset is to build trust, respect, and credibility. The challenge: we can lose all three of those aspects in seconds—after taking years to build them. The key is to intentionally build trust, respect, and credibility between you and your associates and bosses. For me and other executives I have coached, the key is the intentional decision to be focused on others and not self. Therefore, we must work daily at making that mindset part of our DNA. This is also why I stated from the beginning of this journey: it's about *becoming* a Servant Leader, there is no specific destination. It's a process, not an event.

Yes it takes time to build trust, respect, and credibility, and you can't mandate it. However, today you can make the mental shift and begin down that path—and believe me, others will take notice immediately. In most one-on-one coaching I do with feedback teams, the team notices within days and weeks that something different is taking place. It goes back to becoming the person and leader you want to become. Continually refine your future exciting picture. No time like today!

Summary

The Servant Leader does not hope, think, believe, or try; rather, they are committed to the growth and development of others. The Servant Leader understands that all people are hardwired (temperament) differently, but it impacts how we coach delegate, correct, and inspire. We become a student of others so that we can adjust our styles to be most helpful to others. Finally, we understand that it is up to us to build trust, respect, and credibility to create a desire within others to choose to follow us.

Key Questions

1. *Is helpfulness in your DNA? In a court of law, would there be enough evidence to convict you this day of being helpful?*

2. *Do you make it a priority to study others' temperaments to adjust your leadership style to be most helpful?*

3. *How well do you know your own tendencies? How does that knowledge impact your daily interactions?*

4. *What do you do daily, professionally and personally, to build trust within the relationships you influence the most?*

5. *Are you going to ignore, start, or continue your lifelong journey in becoming a Servant Leader, focused more on others' success than your personal gain?*

CHAPTER 10

Work-Life Balance

*It's not about trying to find something to help you be
a more effective leader. It's about trying to be
a better person. The other will follow.*
– James A. Autry, Practicing Servant Leadership

Work is important; at the end of the day it provides income for you and your family. It allows you to be part of funding various special interests—from political campaigns, neighborhood initiatives, nonprofit organizations, and your local church. Giving is one of life's pleasures, a sense that you are giving back and making a positive difference, potentially worldwide. And remember, it's not just financial resources we have to give—we also have our time and talents.

Having a Servant Leader's perspective on life can make all the difference to you and to many others. Too often in my early business career I thought my focus was on helping others, but my decisions were really for my benefit, self-worth, and ego. Yes, I have regrets due to the wrong focus on what was important. For example, against my wife Colleen's advice, I went ahead and purchased additional Dale Carnegie franchises that were not in close proximity of our home, which increased my travel time during the formative years of our five children. I remember telling my wife to take lots of pictures of the various events I would miss, never realizing that today when I look at those pictures they don't give me joy, but regrets because I wasn't there.

Balance is the Key

One of my mentors, Rod Bartell, introduced me to the X+Y = Value formula. X represents your actual wealth measured in American dollars in your personal net worth. Y represents your total satisfaction of living. When you add those two numbers, you get a value. I remember Rod telling me that my Y value needed to be twenty to thirty times greater than X. Then I was to look back five years and then look ahead five years—what was I going to do to grow both Y values twenty times greater than X? It takes a servant heart to understand how important it is to achieve work-life balance. I needed to be *in* the picture rather than seeing the picture afterward.

For example, I knew a man who had over $2 million in cash in the bank, owned two homes, and five cars with his third wife. Only one of four (the last I knew) children talked to him, he had no friends, was miserable to play golf with, and was not even told when his mother died. Big X, no Y.

I know another man who has one wife, been married for 60 years, and acts like a teenager when he is around her (he proposed to her on their first date). He has a loving family, great friends, travels to see and be with a lifetime of friends, and when I am with him, he is engaging, laughs at what is funny and hurts when his friend hurts. His Y is so big—maybe 50 times greater than X. Just so you get my point, his net worth is in the millions, but only those in his inner circle know it.

The first man was a Level I leader, maybe occasionally Level II. Without question, he was about control and he was going to win no matter what and at whose expense. The second man was a Servant Leader. He was always about helping others, and in his lifetime he helped thousands of people win in life and in business.

It is true I can never get those years back. To be fair, they were great years of learning and I could argue that without those experiences I might not be accomplishing what I am today. Regardless, as I began to shift my thinking and walk down the path to understanding what a Servant Leader does and how to lead, I realized that I want to attend my children and grandchildren's events and enjoy the photos of all of us together and receive great joy because I was present. As a result of my emotional mindset shift, Colleen and I attended all fifty of our son's games when he was playing football at Syracuse. Did I mention that I even attended my niece's wedding in Haiti? Yes!

Here are some practical suggestions for achieving work-life balance:

Plan it. Set SMART: Specific, Measurable, Attainable, Relevant, Time-focused goals.

Be intentional. Balancing your work and home life doesn't happen on its own. You must be purposeful in establishing work-life balance. In most cases, you will need an accountability partner in this area. Remember, the balance is not just from your perspective, it's from your family and friend's perspectives as well.

Make new friends. Friends add value to life; they add new perspectives to thinking and doing things. Friendship forces you to take time to build meaningful relationships.

Travel. Plan your travel. Perhaps buy a vacation package with Marriott if that will force you to travel and see new and different cultures and people. Force yourself to leave your comfort zone surroundings. Refill regularly your emotional bucket.

Make your family and friends a priority. Look for opportunities for your entire family to be together. You may have to compromise, but making memories is worth the effort. We choose to invest dollars into family experiences. Schedule quality time with friends.

Go to lunch every day. Call time out and go to lunch, then hit your personal refresh button. Lunch is also a great time to spend time with family, friends, and co-workers.

Make "alone time" valuable. If possible, schedule time at work to think and accomplish personal tasks. This discipline avoids taking work home and robbing family time. Of course, don't do personal tasks on company time.

Read. Pick your own interest and read something fun, something challenging (always be working on your vocabulary), something inspirational, and something mind-blowing. Yes, you can read several books at a time. For example, I enjoy biographies, historical fiction, legal thrillers, and human interest novels. But I also read business books, constantly expanding my comfort zone.

Be interested in others. If appropriate, notice the name of your waiter or the check-out clerks at stores and exchange a few pleasantries. Or why not expand your network and engage in a brief conversation with people at the market about what they are shopping for...enjoy life and others wherever you are.

Manage your time. Make a list and prioritize the activities or tasks based on importance. Always make the best use of your time.

Budget and plan for fun. Life is short, have fun. Be safe, legal, and considerate of others—but you must plan for fun. Perhaps plan for hobby time. Do more of what you enjoy and makes you laugh. Some fun activities can be expensive, so make sure your budget allows for them. If so, you can enjoy vacations, boating, fishing, hunting, golfing, driving, and eating.

Use weekends and short trips to connect with family and friends. Most people live in a new workweek paradigm; the former 5-2 week (work 5 days, off 2 days) is not as common today. Perhaps your traditional week is unpredictable due to travel or other work schedules. It's ok, still plan short trips for whatever days might be your weekend and enjoy. And don't put off driving several hours if it gets you to family and friends.

Go out to dinner with friends. Make going out to dinner part of your routine, maybe not every week, but one time per month works. Colleen and I have a group of friends, twelve couples or so, who get together every Friday. An email is sent to everyone and those who are in town or can make it, meet at the restaurant. Every other month we meet at someone's home. We always have a Christmas party and usually enjoy a long weekend or week vacation in the summer together.

Date your spouse. Hopefully your spouse either is, or is becoming, your best friend. Go on dates together. Take time to enjoy dinners, movies, bowling, golfing, walking, or going to special events like concerts or games. Spending quality time with the person you love the most is a major key in establishing effective work-life balance and boundaries.

Summary

The Servant Leader's heart is 360 degree in nature; it's not a switch you can turn on when you go to work. Please understand that being a Servant Leader is a 24/7 responsibility and effort. So where does your work-life balance fit? As mentioned previously, the book *What Really Works: Blending the Seven Fs* by Paul Batz and Tim Schmidt really helped me see the natural connections by focusing on the seven Fs—faith, family, friends, finances, fitness, future, fun.

Key Questions

1. *Is your Y value 20 times greater than X value? If not, why? What is your immediate plan to adjust?*

2. *What is your work-life balance plan?*

3. *What is your plan to become more intentional in putting on your Servant Leader lenses?*

4. *What are two things you could start doing, stop doing, keep doing that will be helpful to your family?*

5. *What friends do you need to cherish? Or remove?*

CHAPTER 11

Building a Legacy and Finishing Well

Serving others breaks you free from the shackles of self and
self-absorption that choke out the joy of living.
– James C. Hunter, The Servant

The best advice I ever received on building a legacy and finishing well is: *Finish today well. Then plan and finish tomorrow well, and so forth.* This was taught to my son Sam when he was traveling with his baseball team as a kid from age 10 to 15. Dave Sholly, his coach, always emphasized the next pitch, out, batter, ground ball, fly ball, throw to first, throw to the plate—good or bad it was about being successful in the *next* opportunity. A fun four-letter word…NEXT!

I was working in Northeastern Pennsylvania organizing a public Dale Carnegie class in Hawley. My job was to visit companies and enroll their leaders into a public Dale Carnegie class. I received a lead from a company with great promise. I was to visit the company and meet with the company owner late one afternoon. The challenge I was struggling with enrollments at the time and this call had the potential to bring my enrollment numbers up to respectability. It was in late January, cold, snowy, and I had to drive three hours to meet with the man.

From the moment I arrived, on time, things started to go wrong. For starters, he had forgotten about the meeting, and told me he would be right in. But 90 minutes later, approaching 6 p.m., he poked his head in and suggested I read about his company in the latest newsletter, while he would take just a few minutes to eat dinner with his family. Forty-five minutes later, when I had my coat on ready to leave, he reemerged and suggested we speak for a couple of minutes. Then he told me about the latest greatest pyramid business that he thought I would be perfect for. After thirty minutes I excused myself, drove down his lane, got out of my car, and shouted to the hills…"NEXT!"

The good news is the next afternoon I met the owners of a business who not only saved my current class, but became life customers; we are still working together almost twenty years later. Having the mindset of a servant leader today, will help build a lasting legacy for your future.

The challenge in developing a strategy to finish well is that no one knows when you are finished. We have lived long enough to know life can end in a moment, with no apparent bias toward age, gender, social status, wealth, and desires. Yes, you can hedge your bets, eat well, exercise, choose healthy lifestyle choices, but random acts of violence or natural, unexpected events earthquakes, hurricanes, or car accidents can take a life quickly.

So the question is, why live for today and plan for something that you might not ever experience? Answer, it's not about you, it's about and for others. How can you make your life count in such a way that you continue to impact others from the grave? Perhaps remembering you will impact future generations.

John D. Rockefeller has been dead for more than eighty years, yet he continues to impact lives through his investments in colleges and universities that have led to clean water, public sewer systems, medical breakthroughs that save thousands of lives, and many other worthy endeavors he chose to invest in. He laid the groundwork and structure from which men and women from all walks of life today can enjoy and benefit. Yes, his giving was intentional; he could see life long into the future and that focal length continues to change lives for the betterment of the world.

I think of the ancient Jewish writing from the Talmud that had this paraphrased quote I often use with leaders:

> *The world knows of ten strong things:*
> *Iron is strong but fire can melt it*
> *Fire is strong but water can douse it*
> *Water is strong but the sun can evaporate it*
> *The sun is strong but clouds can cover it*
> *Clouds are strong but the wind is stronger*
> *Wind is strong but humans can build shelters*
> *Man is strong but fear can cast him down*
> *Fear is strong but death will end fear*
> *Death is strong but strongest of all is*
> *Kindness for its remembrance can live forever.*

It's not about you! Legacy and finishing well is the example for others to achieve greater success in their chosen fields and endeavors. It's not so you will be remembered for ego purposes; it's the example that truly teaches.

The following is adapted from a story in the book *The Star Thrower* by Loren Eiseley:

> An old man was walking on the beach early one morning.
>
> In the distance, he could see someone moving like a dancer.
>
> As he came closer, he saw that it was a young woman picking up starfish and gently throwing them into the ocean. "Young lady, why are you throwing starfish into the ocean?"
>
> "The sun is up. The tide is going out, and if I do not throw them in they will die," she said.
>
> "But young lady, do you not realize that there are many miles of beach and thousands of starfish? You cannot possibly make a difference."
>
> The young woman listened politely, then bent down, picked up another starfish and threw it into the sea.
>
> "It made a difference for that one."

The question is, in your world will you choose to make a difference?

When our daughter Alexandra graduated from physician's assistant school, all five of our children decided to get a starfish tattoo because the story was told in our home so often as they were growing up. Although I'm not a fan of tattoos, I came to terms with that one because it was so meaningful to us all.

Now that we understand the importance of a legacy and finishing well, the following are some suggestions for how to become future-focused:

- Always be curious; be fascinated with people and their lives, which helps us maintain a learning attitude.
- Always be thinking and responding to people using good human relations. –Dale Carnegie's 30 Human Relation Principles
- Plan your transition to retirement, what you want to do in your retirement years. Perhaps it's 30 years out, but start planning now.
- Read biographies; be a student of others' successes and failures.
- Continue to grow in the seven Fs (Faith, Family, Finance, Fitness, Friends, Future, Fun).
- Find a new passion; always look forward to keep your mind active and alert. Don't allow yourself to plateau when you are in your 30s or 40s.
- Make family activities and events a priority.
- Volunteer to serve, not lead. Our family participated in a mission trip to Haiti and worked on various projects in two orphanages. We helped any way we could, which included moving tables and chairs, painting, digging ditches, and moving rocks. It was a great feeling of accomplishment and fulfillment.
- Dale Carnegie teaches to expect ingratitude; in fact, receiving a thank you is not the reason we give—we give to be helpful and loving toward others.

Eight Habits of a Servant Leader

Habit 1 – Be a Learner

Desire to learn all you can. When I was a senior in high school, my dad took me out to prune some walnut trees. Talk about legacy! These walnut trees might be harvested by my great-grandchildren. We were taking a break mid-morning when my dad made a claim I called him on. He said, "Son, I can tell you with great preciseness how tall each of the 400-plus walnut trees will grow this year." Well, I knew just enough biology to know that this might turn into an easy lunch. I said, "Dad, no way. I bet you lunch." To my surprise and delight, he took me up on my bet. To emphasize his point and to have a bit of fun, Dad walked around rubbing his chin making a few marks in a pocket notebook, and then returned to where I was sitting and said, "I got it…each tree will grow as tall as it can." He went on to explain that he believed despite our mistakes in pruning and the wind, rain, snow, ice, etc., he was confident he was right. Then he said, "I wonder what would happen if we had the same attitude toward learning?"

Habit 2 – Set Goals

Have you noticed that people who do not set goals usually achieve them? Nothing. Can you imagine an airplane pilot who has no idea where he or she is going? I was taking the red-eye to Pittsburgh one night when the pilot announced, "Enjoy the flight, sleep well, and we'll talk again on our descent into Miami." We all woke up! I guess the only thing worse would be not knowing where we were taking off from. Yet we at times fail to set goals in our lives and careers and then wonder how we ended up where we are. Again, shift your mindset from setting goals for yourself to what would be most helpful to others. Coaching a third-generation business transition can be challenging as the current leader, the father in this case, does not believe in setting goals, he believes it's too restrictive. How do you think that is working for the next generation?

Habit 3 – Be an Encourager

Being an encourager is the heart of motivation for the Servant Leader. Not only is it the most positive attitude you can have toward others, it also picks you up when you are feeling most challenged. Think about it for just a moment there are so many ways to encourage others in what you say, do, write, respond, and celebrate.

Habit 4 – Train Yourself

Train yourself to be the best at what you do on planet Earth. Servant Leaders challenge themselves not to be recognized as the best, but to better serve others. You will be challenged as a Servant Leader if you are not trusted in your field of expertise. You will be making strong, powerful statements to others based on your continuous learning attitude.

Habit 5 – Select Good Mentors and Coaches

Who do you choose to hang out with? Individuals who build you up or people who drain you? This is your choice. Somewhere in my travels I heard a speaker say that your mentors should always have four times your own net worth and be ten years older or wiser. The reason is that they will most likely think differently and have had more experiences that you. Gale Rickner, until his death at age 85, was a mentor of mine, and I would see him maybe twice a year. The last time I saw him, we were out for dinner and I asked him, "Of all that life has taught you, what was currently top of mind?"

He said, "Johnny, when I was in my 40s, I used to worry about what others were saying about me. When I hit my 60s, I gained perspective in that I know longer cared what others were saying about me. And now that I'm in my 80s, I have gained even more insight into human nature, realizing that during all those years, no one was even thinking about me, let alone talking about me, because they were too worried about their own lives." After a good laugh, we went on to discuss some of my perceived fears of what might be holding me back from achieving my business and family goals.

My father frequently shared this notable quote:

Small people talk about people.
Average people talk about things.
Extraordinary people talk about concepts and ideas.

I made a decision a long time ago that if at all possible, I was going to choose to hang around with extraordinary people.

Habit 6 – Be Enthusiastic

Choosing to *be* enthusiastic every day is important. I love the word "be"—and which part of the word are we struggling with. Often, two-letter words are the most powerful in the English language. I have been taught that "enthusiasm" is the Greek root word that means "God within." Although I'm fine with the dictionary definition: intense and eager enjoyment, interest, or approval. It's not necessarily loud energy, although based on some people's temperament it may be exercised that way. With the Servant Leader lens, I see enthusiasm as more quiet confidence, which is seen in the eyes and in the sense of purpose that you or another person is expressing.

Mike Norman, whose family operates the Dale Carnegie franchise in Minnesota, defined enthusiasm to me just by watching him walk into a room. I wanted to follow him just from seeing how enthusiastic he was. Why is enthusiasm a habit for the Servant Leader? It instills in others a sense of confidence and belief that with the right attitude they and others can achieve the impossible.

Habit 7 – Be a Possibility Thinker

Why not be a possibility thinker? There surely are enough naysayers in our world. Let us express the confidence that all things are possible. Instead of saying no to a crazy idea, why not say, "That's interesting, tell me what you are thinking." Servant Leaders take time to just think. Too often we get caught up in the notion that if we aren't speaking or doing something, we aren't being productive. Thinking is working. Thinking what might be possible is working hard. Be a disrupter in thought...hear yourself thinking, *I wonder what would happen if we...*

Habit 8 – Be the Model Servant Leader

What you *do* shouts so loudly I cannot *hear* what you say. Become other-focused, shift your mindset from "me" to "we." Be more supportive rather than directive in your coaching and unlocking the abilities of others. Make the servant mindset your default leadership style, your new leadership DNA. Be helpful and loving toward others; help others win in life and work. Realize that if you help others win, you will be leading a fulfilling life with manageable stress and a loving family.

Summary

I heard a statistic that only one out of three leaders will finish well. You need to master the art of stretching your focal length to see the future and how you might continue to influence and impact lives long after you have passed from this existence.

Key Questions

1. *How long is your focal length?*
2. *What could you begin doing today to take your focal length out 10, 20, 50 years?*
3. *What is your daily plan to become more thankful, appreciative, and kind?*
4. *Who are the extraordinary people in your life, and what is your plan to hang around with them more or to find additional extraordinary friends?*
5. *What would it mean to you, co-workers, friends, and family if you choose today to become the model Servant Leader?*

Chapter 12

The Servant Leader's Professional and Personal Game Plan

The only ones among you who will be really happy are those who will have sought and found how to serve.
– James C. Hunter, The Servant

Planning is a constant and important theme for becoming the Servant Leader. There are many planning models, and most can be used as helpful guides. A few keys in any planning model is making sure you spend enough time on identifying and defining what you want to bring into existence—and making sure everyone is seeing the same picture. Then follow up with the factual, realistic picture of the current state. Often a move is made too quickly, before everyone is on the same page.

When vacationing with family in a foreign country, several of the guys wanted to rent a sea-doo jet ski. English was not the first language of the person we were renting from, so when we asked how far we could go, he said, "As far as the eye can see." A couple of our guys jumped on the jet ski and took off around the coast. Our renter actually meant as far as *his* eyes could see, and we watched him chase down the guys as they zoomed out of sight. Clear language and understanding is important.

The next thing in a good planning model needs to be the back-up plan, because a single plan seldom goes as smoothly; something unexpected always comes up. Mike Tyson, the famous boxer, is credited for saying, "Everyone has a good plan, until they get hit in the nose." So, what are your contingency plans?

The following are four steps to follow when writing your game plan:

Servant Leader Game Plan

Step One: Vision. Who are you busy becoming as a leader?

This activity describes a future, exciting picture of who you are becoming as a Servant Leader. Using powerful words, envision who is responding to you and how you feel about their successes, not yours (200-300 words). Hint: write something about becoming more servant-like and less commanding and controlling.

I am: _____

_____

_____

_____

_____

_____

_____

_____

_____

_____

_____

Step Two: Create a simple *Structural Tension Chart* for your department or team (adapted from Robert Fritz's book *The Path of Least Resistance for Managers*, pages 27-41.)

	When thinking about your team, department, or division, what do you want to do or create? Think of 2-4 future SMART goals (Specific, Measurable, Applicable, Realistic, Time frame).
1.	
2.	
3.	
4.	
	For each of the goals stated above, assess its current reality/state using facts.
1.	
2.	
3.	
4.	

	Strategies/Actions that need to be taken to move from reality to desired results	Time frame	People Names to be held accountable	Task and activities that need to be developed or coached
1.				
2.				
3.				
4.				
5.				
6.				

Step 3 – Serving and Growing Others' Game Plan

Name- Who on my team do we need to develop?	List the task or activities we need to develop.	Performance Standards- Describe what success looks like.	Determine which of the 6 stages of development will we start at for each task.	What will be my Human Relations strategy? Dale Carnegie wrote 30	Accoun- tability Strategy
	1. 2. 3. 4.				
	1. 2. 3. 4.				
	1. 2. 3. 4.				
	1. 2. 3. 4.				

Step Four – Personal Development Chart

Do Less	Do More	Do Different

Tension Chart Instructions. Note: You want to create tension between the outcomes or goals you desire and the current reality. When you are challenged with what you want versus what is, your mind naturally goes to determining what you have to do to bring into existence your future state. According to Robert Fritz, this tension creates clarity. For the Servant Leader, this process defines what we now need to do to be helpful to our team. Now we can lead.

Next, what specific actions will you take to move you from your current state to your desired outcome, which is to function more as a Servant Leader? Action steps may be with yourself, current team, family, or others. Perhaps your actions step will be more goal-oriented. Perhaps apply human relation principles with more discipline, maybe changing up how and when you communicate. Regardless, if you want to be more of a Servant Leader, the actions should come quickly and be obvious.

Next, all actions need to be timed-stamped and then select a person or persons to hold you accountable. Note: it could be a different person for each action. Finally, list the tasks and activities you need to coach the individual to complete the strategy to achieve the desired results.

Game Plan Chart Instructions. Starting with the name of the associate you will be leading, write that name in column one. Then when thinking about this person, what are the tasks or activities that this person needs to improve? Note: It is suggested that you write up to four possible tasks or activities. Could be less, might be more. For each task or activity, you must determine what good looks like; in Dale Carnegie's Leadership Training for Managers course, we call these performance standards. Then you need to choose which development stage you will start with, then which corresponding human relation principle will give you the best leverage to create a win-win in being helpful to the associate and aiding the person's success.

The final step is to think clearly about your accountability strategy. Perhaps it's as simple as adopting one of the five steps of leadership and accountability outlined in a previous chapter. Or taking a deeper dive into one or more of the strategies in Level IV and V. Please review the Accountability Chart.

Personal Development Chart Instructions. After reading this book, choosing to follow the path of a servant leader and taking into consideration your answers to the Key Questions, what might you consider doing more of, doing less of, or do differently in your life today? Make a list and get started.

Summary

Do you have such a plan? Most leaders wing it and hope for the best. What if you could learn to be more intentional in how you serve others? Here lies the heart of accountability: having a plan that everyone agrees with and has clear expectations, milestones, goals, action steps, and resource allocations with contingencies mapped out. Only now can you hold yourself and others accountable.

Key Questions

1.   *What is your game plan?*

2.   *What is one thing you could do to begin or continue the process of becoming a Servant Leader?*

3.   *How might you become more intentional and purposeful in helping others achieve their goals?*

4.   *What is your Servant Leader accountability strategy to achieve intended results?*

5.   *Can you imagine developing a personal game plan for every person in your life whom you can directly influence?*

Conclusion

Onward and Upward

*The challenge of servant leadership is to be strong,
but not rude; be bold, but not timid; be proud,
but not arrogant; have humor, but without folly.*
– Jim Rohn

Put on Your Servant Glasses

I dare you! I dare you to change how you think, work, and play. It starts by seeing the world through a different lens. Put on your Servant Leader glasses and watch how everything you thought about management and leadership changes. To go deeper, observe how every aspect of your life changes, every relationship, goals, and aspirations—all will be altered in a positive, impactful, life-changing way.

If you refuse the dare, my fear is that you might choose to do nothing. Perhaps you, like me, think you already understand the servant mindset and it might be good for someone else you know, but not for you. I dare you for one day to analyze every thought and decision you make to apply the Servant Leader filter: *Is this about me for my benefit or is it about helping others succeed?* The filter is based on other people's point of view of how your decisions are helping *them* with *their* success.

There is an old story often told about a ship that is in the harbor all ready to set sail. It is filled with goods and products to stock many store shelves, and ultimately the goods will find their way into hundreds of homes. The captain is on the bridge, contemplating all the risks of setting sail. He thought, *We may have to sail into bad weather, perhaps we might get lost, maybe hit an iceberg, run out of fuel, and even attacked by pirates. Ah, but consider the happiness and joy by setting sail and arriving at our destination and the commerce that will take place; that outweighs the negative, potential consequences.* Then he was reminded by his old sea captain who had remained his mentor that the greatest risk was to do nothing; not set sail, just stay in the harbor, and eventually the boat will rot and decay and sink to the harbor floor.

Doing nothing about becoming a Servant Leader leads us and others nowhere. To think we don't need it or already have it or it's for someone else might be a devastating blow to how you finish in life. Finding contentment in work and life by embracing the core principals of being a Servant Leader allow us to win and move to higher levels in every aspect of our lives. Remember, it is never about the destination of the perfect state of being a servant…hint, you will never get there. Rather, it is the true joy of the trip in becoming and transforming yourself in being more servant-like. It is a process not an event.

The following Table illustrates a sampling of management tools and the shift in thinking when you put on servant lenses and focus on others. The following is an example of when you choose to see the world through servant lenses and everything changes.

My point of view is that life is too short not to grow in our capacity to help and love others. Also, it is not about big changes— the little things and adjustments make the biggest difference. Think of when you nudge the station knob on your old radio that made the fuzzy voice come in loud and clear. Or how a pen running out of ink skips portions of letters as you write and how a new pen glides ink clearly for each letter across the page.

Management Tool	Command and Control *"Me"*	Servant Leader *"We"*
Planning	A process so others know what to do for me.	A process to cover all the bases to help others know what good looks like for our success.
Innovation/ Problem Solving	A process to solve critical issues to better my objectives and to keep others out of my office to save time and advance progress.	A process that is helpful to others to find and advance solutions to problems while developing our team problem solving skills to create win-win results for our customers.
Motivation	A technique to get people to accomplish what I need from them by doing more with fewer resources in a faster, positive, inspiring way.	A technique that helps others achieve successes by creating an environment that equips them to do more with less faster and brings others along in a positive, inspiring way.
Delegating	A technique to remove tasks from my desk to yours so I can work on more meaningful duties.	A technique to build others, to unleash talents of my team members with a process that holds them and myself accountable for results. Also, helps them grow to their next level of performance.
Coaching	A process to develop skills to benefit my success in the development of my team.	A process that is helpful to others in advancing skills and abilities for their benefit and professional development.
Accountability	A technique to give clear expectations and consequences of non-performance if they fail me.	A technique that holds us 100% responsible to each other for the results. Then clearly define how together we will achieve what needs to be done for the benefits of others combined with a "'We' will not fail" attitude.
Corrective Action	A process to communicate with clarity what the issues are, where they failed [me] and exactly what needs to be done to restore the relationship with me. Gives them a deadline and the consequences if their behavior is not corrected by that deadline.	A process to be helpful to others in their personal and professional development. Get the facts, ask questions to seek further understanding using human relations to help them identify with the mistake, restore the relationship, and communicate that you are a continuous resource for future questions and concerns.

Putting on the servant lens and seeing life anew is that easy, just a small adjustment, yet it changes everything. Decisions that were so hard to make become crystal clear. Broken relationships are now easy to mend. New goals and actions are easily seen and understood. Our communications become clearer and more easily comprehended. Followers follow dreams and they become reality. When we choose to wear our Servant Leader lenses and we see more clearly what our aspirations are in helping others achieve their success, it becomes very clear what we need to do more of, what we need to do less of, and what we need to do differently.

Closing Q&A

What do I need to do first?

- Continually update your vision of who you are becoming.

What should I commit to doing every morning?

- Determine to be intentional; put on your servant lenses before getting out of bed.
- Commit to the three BEs:
    1. Be thankful;
    2. Be appreciative;
    3. Be kind.

What do I need to remind myself of throughout the day?

- Am I influencing others by shifting my responses, beliefs, and paradigms to better serve others?
- When faced with difficult situations, always ask yourself, *What is the wise thing to do that would be helpful and loving toward others?*
- When frustrated or angry, shift your thinking from "me" to "we."

What do I need to do after work and every night?

- Keep the lenses on for the people you love the most.
- Sleep well, for when tomorrow comes, you will make it a great day!

Closing Actions

1. Write down what you will choose to do. What's not written, does not exist.
2. Let others know what you are trying to accomplish; go together.
3. Gather your team to develop a servant culture to maximize results.
4. Call me, I'm willing to help!

Most importantly: commit to this simple mindset of making others successful by putting on your Servant Leader lenses!

Onward!

One Last Story

Touring the Cruzan Rum Distillery in Saint Croix, I was amazed to learn about the process of making rum. During the tour, our guide explained that rum was made with the simple mixture of rain water, yeast, and molasses. Gallons and gallons of molasses.

Of the 100,000 gallons we saw boiling, we were told only 10 percent of it would be distilled that would result in the product of the rum we drink or cook with. The majority, 90 percent, becomes a byproduct used in other ways, including feed for animals. The 10 percent that rises to the top is put into fifty-five gallon barrels to age. The finest rum ages for twelve years; and to my amazement, only five gallons of pure rum is left after evaporation takes place. On the island, they call it feeding the angels.

This reminds me of what it takes to rise to the highest level of leadership—as a Servant Leader whose sole desire is unlocking the abilities of others. So few make it...about 10 percent of the people who either desire or have the talent or skill to become a leader, only a few through an aging and experience process can make the emotional shift from "me" to "we" to become a Servant leader, like rum making, like servant leader, is a process, not an event.

Appendix A
Recent History of the Servant Leader

Robert K. Greenleaf, in an essay written in 1970, re-coined the modern-day term Servant Leader in his essay, *The Servant as Leader*. And it was Isaac Newton who was credited with saying, "If I can see so far ahead, it's because I stand on the shoulders of giants." I often wondered when reading this quote, *Who were those giants?* More importantly, how did they purposefully and intentionally become giants who served others so well? More on Robert K. Greenleaf at the conclusion of this appendix.

A question I like to ask executive groups that always seems to stump modern thinkers is, what must a leader have? The rather simple but powerful answer is *followers*. Followers must be led by their choice. Followership cannot be mandated. Through service, the Servant Leader attracts followers like a giant magnet: the ultimate in achieving the "It" factor. Leaders who have a presence when they are with others, have "it." In fact, others naturally want to follow those with the "it" factor—a sense of self-awareness and confidence that others can sense faster than they can observe.

When studying servant leadership, we will never find a human being who has achieved perfection—nor is it necessarily our goal for those of us desiring to become Servant Leaders to achieve perfection. In fact, I would say forget it, as today's Servant Leaders, like all humans, are imperfect. President Abraham Lincoln put this way, "Still, if we have learned anything since ancient times, which is debatable when it comes to moral advancement, it's that we are now wise enough to know that each and every one of us, to varying degrees, has both admirable and undesirable qualities."

So to study servant leadership, we must look to when individuals demonstrated service above self for a period of time, a season of life, or in a moment of brilliance. Perhaps you might have recognized Rotary International's key phrase, "Service above self." Paul Harris, one of the founders of Rotary International, is a great example of servant leadership. However, those who knew Harris also recognized his challenges and actions that might seem less than servant-like. My point is simple: look for people who are great examples of service in becoming less self-centered and more selfless on behalf of others.

Early Leadership Philosophers

Not to bore you to death but to give perspective, the earliest known writers of leadership style are found in the Far East. Chinese philosopher Lao-Tzu in the 6th century BC advocated a selflessness trait in a leader and promoted a non-directive leadership style. In the West, Greek philosophers, Socrates and Aristotle, are given credit for writing about followership during the 4th century BC.

Around 30 BC, a new leader was talked about in ancient writings, Jewish writings, and in the Bible what became known as the New Testament. Jesus of Nazareth lived a life of approximately 33 years and his servant's heart continues to influence and impact millions 2,000 years after his death. Regardless, of your religious beliefs, the descriptions of Jesus's actions help us see more clearly what a selflessness life and its impact has on influencing and unleashing others. For example, did you know Jesus actually washed the feet of the very man who later betrayed him, leading directly to his death? Jesus unleashed a movement that 2,000 years later continues to grow and flourish with at the center of its core beliefs is to love others.

Other religious leaders also follow a belief in servanthood. Mohammad, Confucius, and Buddha all taught their followers, in their writings and teachings, the power in serving others. However, servant leadership expands beyond religious beliefs and teachings, and it would be a shame to dismiss servant leadership as a religious belief without any other credible stakeholders. Without getting into too much detail, let's examine just a few.

Servant leadership philosophies continued through the Middles Ages with the writings of St. Thomas Aquinas (1225-1274), Christine de Pizan (1364-1430), Niccolo Machiavelli (1469-1527), Sir Francis Bacon (1561-1626), and Thomas Hobbes (1588-1679). During the Enlightenment Period leadership philosophy writers include: John Locke, David Hume, Adam Smith, Voltaire, Jean-Jacques Rousseau, Denis Diderot, Paine, Mary Wollstonecraft. All wrote philosophies about various aspects of serving others.

This then leads us to the German philosopher Georg Hegel (1770-1831) who perhaps gave us the greatest insights to a paradigm shift surrounding the relationship of the follower, servant, and leader. In America emerged Ralph Waldo Emerson (1803-1882), a philosopher who helped redefine the relationship between a servant and a Servant Leader.

In the early 1900s emerged onto the American business scene and soon the global scene was a farmer from Missouri who left his family farm in search of riches, Dale Carnegie. In 1936, after returning home from a summer speaking tour in Europe, he finished writing and publishing *How to Win Friends and Influence People* in which Carnegie wrote about thirty human relation principles on how to lead with another focus to best unleash and influence others for their good and for their successes. This was the first "how to" book ever published and jump-started the multibillion-dollar business of personal and professional development. For the first time, people around the world could be trained in how to become a Servant Leader. Interestingly enough, most people who have read the book loved it, but still missed the point in applying the principles as a way to serve others rather than a way to achieve personal gain.

Emerson, Carnegie, and others led to Peter Drucker, the father of modern management, who separated the disciplines of management and leadership and quoted other philosophers that leaders lead people and should have a goal of being a servant to others.

This leads us back to Robert Greenleaf's servant leadership breakthrough-thinking in 1970. Greenleaf wrote volumes about servant leadership with several articles published from his notes and essays after his death in 1990. This brings us to 2001 when the concept of servant leadership or Level V leadership has reemerged, greatly due to two factors.

Current Leadership Philosophers

First, Jim Collins's book *Good to Great* popularized the term "Level V leadership" when he and his research staff studied hundreds of companies to define the entities that went from good to great. Collins identified and studied eleven such corporations over a fifteen-year period. All eleven of the companies that met the financial criteria were led by a Level V leader, whom we will also call a Servant Leader. Collins wrote about the leadership styles of companies that moved from good to great; each seemed to have what he termed Level V leadership. Jim writes that the Level V leader "seems to be steeped in humility but with unwavering will." This identification has caught the thought patterns of thousands of leaders in asking what that looks like.

Second, as of 2016, there are approximately 75 million millennials in the United States workforce. The millennials in 2016 were ages 21-34 and are already the most productive generation ever: they refuse to be micromanaged (Level I or II), they want to be led (Levels IV and V), or they just leave. They crave the Level V or Servant Leader who is willing to communicate in "why" and not just "what" needs to be done. They crave to be turned loose on a project with collaborative efforts and with a leader who is helpful but not overbearing. Leaders of millennials better talk about the "why" game if they want their people to bring their "A" game to the workplace.

The core leadership issue is how to become more helpful and less controlling? What does it look like now in the 21st century in the midst of global economic and political chaos combined with information overload?

Today we can learn about servant leadership in biographies and by watching for executives who have a long view in serving others. Perhaps in the short term they may have been misunderstood, but history illustrates the heart of a servant. After reading their biographies, the following are a few very successful individuals who demonstrated a service mindset: the Wright Brothers, Vince Lombardi, Tom Landry, John D. Rockefeller, Billy Graham, Harry S. Truman, John Adams, Thomas Jefferson, Norman Vincent Peale, and Dale Carnegie.

While much has been written on this concept, little has been written on the "how" to become a servant leader. As a result of my personal executive coaching, keynote addresses I present, and leading senior leadership discussions, I keep hearing, "John, this was insightful and interesting. Where can I read more about your servant leadership observations?" Because I didn't have a good answer, I was encouraged by my senior leadership team to start writing—this book is one of many to be released, in hopes of helping others.

Onward!

Summary

The Servant Leader has a long history, going back maybe as early as 2000 BC and can be identified in leaders as early as there is recorded written history. The point being, servant leadership is not new and the purpose of this book was not to sell people on the relevance of servant leadership over command-and-control leadership. Rather, the purpose is to stay focused on the core theme of what it takes to become a servant leader in today's world. Then to have the discipline to put on your servant lenses often (daily, hourly) to become about others—and remember it's not about you—it's about others.

Recommended Reading

Dale Carnegie, *How to Win Friends and Influence People*

Dale Carnegie, *How to Stop Worrying and Start Living*

Dale Carnegie, *How to Win Friends & Influence People in the Digital Age*

Paul Batz and Tim Schmidt, *What Really Works*

Bob Buford, *Finishing Well:What People Who Really Live Do Differently*

Larry Bossidy and Ram Charan, *Execution: The Discipline of Getting Things Done*

Ron Chernow, *Alexander Hamilton*

Ron Chernow, *Titan: John D. Rockefeller Sr.*

Jim Collins, *Good to Great: Why Some Companies Make the Leap and Others Don't*

Jim Collins and Jerry I. Porras, *Built to Last: Successful Habits of Visionary Companies*

Steve Covey, *The 7 Habits of Highly Effective People*

Richard Ben Cramer, *Joe Dimaggio*

Jeffrey E. Garten, *The Mind of the CEO*

Marshall Goldsmith, *MOJO: How to Get It, How to Keep It, How to Get it Back if You Lose It*

Marshall Goldsmith, *What Got You Here Won't Get You There*

Vern Harnish, *Mastering the Rockefeller Habits*

Vern Harnish, *Scaling Up: How a Few Companies Make It...and Why the Rest Don't*

Bryce Hoffman, *American Icon: Alan Mulally and the Fight to Save Ford Motor Company*

Chet Holmes, *The Ultimate Sales Machine: Turbocharge Your Business with Relentless Focus*

Walter Isaacson, *Steve Jobs*

Daniel Kahneman, *Thinking, Fast and Slow*

Bob Kelleher, *Louder than Words: Harness the Power of Your Authentic Voice*

W. Chan Kim & Renee Mauborgne, *Blue Oceans Strategy*

Phil Knight, *Shoe Dog: A Memoir by the Creator of Nike*

Charles Leerhsen, *Ty Cobb: A Terrible Beauty*

Michael Lewis, *The Undoing Project: A Friendship that Changed Our Minds*

David Maraniss, *When Pride Still Mattered: A Life of Vince Lombardi*

Michael MacCambridge, *Chuck Noll: His Life's Work*

Harvey MacKay, *Swim with the Sharks*

Og Mandino, *University of Success*

John C. Maxwell, *The 21 Irrefutable Laws of Leadership*

David McCullough, *The Wright Brothers*

David McCullough, *Truman*

Tom Peters, *In Search of Excellence: Lessons from America's Best-Run Companies*

Daniel Pink, *Drive: The Surprising Truth About What Motivates Us*

Mark Ribowsky, *The Last Cowboy: Tom Landry*

Andy Stanley, *Visioneering*

Gordon R. Sullivan and Michael V. Harper, *Hope is Not a Method: What Business Leaders Can Learn from America's Army*

Rick Warren, *The Purpose Driven Life*

Gino Wickman, *Traction: Get a Grip on Your Business*

Gino Wickman and Mark C. Winters, *Rocket Fuel: The One Essential Combination that Will Get You More of what You Want from Your Business*

John Wooden, *My Personal Best*

About the Author

John Rodgers serves as a senior executive coach to multiple high-profile companies and global organizations. He is the owner and president of Dale Carnegie Systems. John is internationally recognized for his ability to coach senior-level leaders on critical Level 5 Leadership strategies and tactics, enhancing executive image and engagement, as well as advanced communication skills for high-profile leaders. He is renowned for reducing collateral damage among senior staffs and connecting top-level executives with their management teams.

John recently completed a highly successful term as president of the International Dale Carnegie Franchise Association. He worked with 180 franchises in various change management initiatives, business modeling, contract adjustments, and new business growth opportunities.

John has been with Dale Carnegie for more than 28 years. For nearly a decade, he coached and worked side by side with presidents, senior vice presidents, and C-level executives of large, well-established organizations to improve their overall effectiveness in working through people and being perceived by others as confident, poised, and professional senior-level leaders.

John is a graduate of Pennsylvania State University and earned a Master's degree from Shippensburg University. John and his wife, Colleen, have five adult children and two granddaughters. John and Colleen live in State College, Pennsylvania.

Notes :

_____

_____

_____

_____

_____

_____

_____

_____

_____

_____

_____

_____

_____

_____

_____

_____

Lightning Source UK Ltd.
Milton Keynes UK
UKHW022008090819
347710UK00016B/434/P